Advance praise f

Aphrod

You walk the reader through such a huge range of emotions, in such an intimate way—it is incredible. And your use of analogies is brilliant!

Valerie Ciccone

I was so impressed with your book excerpts. They really resonate with where life seems to be at this age.

Robh Ruppel

I read all the excerpts. Some were sad; some were happy, and all of them were filled with a depth and complexity of meaning some people just can't imagine. Wow...All of them were wonderful, beautiful, and intriguing.

Jasmine Dahilig

Napalm Incident is laugh-out-loud hilarious—Erica Jong meets Margaret Cho.

Marc Beauchamp

My daughter gave me a sample of your book, it is very insightful. Even at my age, 78, I remember those years.

Rosemary Agabra

Really funny stuff. Let the truth be told!

Neal Walk

Aphrodite *in* Jeans

Adventure Tales about Men, Midlife and Motherhood

Katherine Shirek Doughtie

Copyright © 2005 Katherine Shirek Doughtie

Portions of the material also appear on www.aphroditeinjeans.com
© 2005 by Katherine Shirek Doughtie. All rights reserved.

All names have been changed to protect the innocent (and otherwise). No part of this publication may be reproduced, stored in a retrieval system or transmitted in any form or by any means electronic, mechanical, photocopying, recording or otherwise, without the prior written consent of the publisher.

For information, please contact:
Haven Books
10153½ Riverside Drive, Suite 629
North Hollywood, CA 91602
www.havenbooks.net

Library of Congress Cataloging-In-Publication Data:

Doughtie, Katherine Shirek.
Aphrodite in jeans : adventure tales about men, midlife and motherhood /- Katherine Shirek Doughtie.

p. ; cm.
ISBN-13 : 978-1-58436-800-7
ISBN-10 : 1-58436-800-4

1. American essays. 2. Middle aged women—Attitudes.
3. Middle aged women—Conduct of life. 4. Motherhood.
5. Man-woman relationships. I. Title.

PS3554.O8215 A64 2005
814/.54 2005928523

Library of Congress Control Number: 2005928523
Copy Editors: Dorthea Atwater, Cynthia Johnston and Faye Docuyanan
Special thanks to Bridget Agabra Goldstein

Visit our website at www.aphroditeinjeans.com

Printed in the United States of America
First printing 2005

To Chris and Jack

Table of Contents

Bonus Tracks

Aphrodite *in* Jeans

Adventure Tales about Men, Midlife and Motherhood

Introduction: The Path with Heart

I *woke up one day* in my early forties and realized I was halfway through the time I was going to spend on this planet. My wallet of temporal currency was dwindling; it was imperative I start spending the rest of it as mindfully as possible.

These are stories that grew out of that moment of truth. They have to do with being single, in mid-life, a mother of two growing boys, and the daughter of an aging father. These are adventure stories, random thoughts and oddball connections. These are conversations I would have with a girlfriend on a long road trip, or with old friends over the remains of dinner as we laugh long into the night.

Looking back, I see that my moment of clarity was actually a call to adventure. Everyone receives such a call at least once in a lifetime. It's possible that call happens once a day, even once an hour. It doesn't take a hero to answer that call. But only a fool ignores it.

Calls to adventure are ignored at one's own risk, and we all eventually end up going down our pre-appointed roads anyway. There are repeated chances in this life because destiny will prevail. Destiny *wants* to happen. It will come at its own time and in its own way.

Is everything a call to adventure? Obviously it's important to have some way to differentiate calls to adventure from plain old stupid ideas. Blind lust is sometimes a herald to the call to adventure, but sometimes it's simply blind lust. How to tell the difference?

Carlos Castaneda talks about the path with heart as the path you will know as the right one if you strip away all fear and ambition. One of the ways I try to figure out if I'm on the right track is to ask myself—without fear or ambition—whether it's the path with heart. The answer is always immediately apparent. What I do with that knowledge is up to me.

Following the path with heart takes guts. It's like hurtling down a wild unknown river, without a life preserver or paddle. Sometimes one part of the journey becomes so lovely that I can't possibly imagine life ever getting better. So I fight furiously against the current, trying to stay still as long as possible so I can hold on to that one place. And while I'm expending all that energy, I'm missing every possibility around the next bend.

Sometimes during a turbulent patch I lose all belief that calm waters will eventually return. I freeze or I freak out or I panic and flail. Sometimes I find myself utterly exhausted and realize I've been doing the equivalent of swimming upstream as hard and fast as I can. Trying to get back to a place that's safe.

No matter how hard the journey, my prayer is that I never lose heart altogether. My greatest fear is to end up banked on the side, growing roots and watching sadly as the river passes by.

This summer I stood on a small bridge overlooking a stream in Vermont. And I had an interesting thought: If I were a leaf floating on that stream, what I'd be most aware of, in fear of, and consumed by would be the *rocks.*

The rocks would always be in my way, forcing me to go one way or the other, making me crazy with their random appearance. I would try like crazy to avoid them, but they would appear in front of me again and again. If I were a leaf, my life would be *all* about the rocks.

When viewed from above, however, the thing that's most interesting about the stream is its direction and flow. It's obvious from the bridge that the rocks have nothing to do with anything. They add beauty. They add texture. But they do *nothing* to impede the leaf's journey. That leaf is traveling downstream, whether it wants to or not.

The obstacles simply do not matter. Even the destination does not matter. The movement, the flow, the act of navigating the waters—that's what it's all about.

Asking yourself—without fear or ambition—if a direction is a path with heart tells you if you're poised on the edge of the right river bank. The call to adventure is the invitation to jump into that river and find out what's going to happen next.

When lobsters grow too large for their shells, they go through an involuntary and desperate struggle to free themselves. That which once protected now confines. They battle their way out only to become completely vulnerable until their exoskeleton hardens again.

When I did the unthinkable and started a conversation that would eventually result in the end of my marriage, I was struggling to break free of a shell that no longer protected me. Since the divorce, I have discovered that it's not only relationships that start off protecting and end up confining. Fear is a shell. Anger is a shell. Thought that does not dare to soar is a shell.

All of these shells are vitally important for a while. Then, as we grow, they keep us from being fully ourselves. We grow at our own pace and strive to connect with other people who are also growing and evolving.

A common theme in this collection is my search for connection—with where I've been, where I am, and where I'm going. I explore my connection to my past as I take care of my father in his last years. I look at my relationship with my children, watching how we interact and what we learn from each other. And I also explore the connectedness between men and women—how we infuriate and mesmerize each other, how we catalyze great life events while at the same time completely disappointing each other in the most minute details.

As I watch my boys grow up, I am continually amazed at how little age really has to do with anything. When we exchange our dreams in the morning, I realize that their nightmares about being chased by the Green Goblin are no different from my dreams of tidal waves. Their worries about being popular in the fifth grade are absolutely the same as mine about whatever boyfriend is around at the moment. Their vocabulary is different but the stories are the same.

Just as my kids are absorbed in stories of Spiderman's secret identity, my dad in his last years was busy developing ever-more elaborate conspiracy theories. He occupied his days doing research in the library and making endless copies of the same documents. As his body began to fail and his speech struggled to find the simple nouns of life, his mind spun webs and concocted elaborate schemes.

In many ways, this is no different from my own continual worry and planning. I, too, create my own scenarios to keep myself busy. I try to make order out of the chaos so I can stay buffered from realities that are too harsh to confront head on: I am aging. I will die.

There will be a moment after which I will never see my children's faces again. There will be a word I write that will be my last word.

It's too much. Too unbearable. For any of us. So my father creates conspiracy theories about why everything's going to hell, I buy potions that guarantee cellulite removal, and my co-workers gather by the coffee machine and struggle with workplace politics. It's OK. It's the thing that living people do. It distracts us. It works.

Several years ago I was in Arizona, heading west through the vast red deserts, bouncing along in a truck carrying theatrical sets. We had finally left the reservation behind us and stopped at Navajo Bridge, an incredible span across the Colorado.

I got out and stood in the middle, looking. There was complete silence except for the churning of the water far below. The river was an incredible green, the shores appeared small and safe, the texture of the current was intricate and serene. Looking upstream, I could see the gorge twist and turn away, the huge cliffs reflecting in the water. The wind blew against my shoulders; the sun warmed my skin.

I rested my chin down on the railing and watched, becoming still. The spirits of the mountains, the wind and the river converged, holding me in their palm.

I prayed.

I prayed to the spirit of the world and the spirit of the universe and the spirit within me. Don't let me go, I implored them. Never let me go. Keep me attuned to the source, listening to the source, connected to the source. Keep me on the river. Hold me and don't let me go.

Give me a partner to share all this wonder with. This is too good a journey to do it alone. I want a spiritual companion—someone to go to these places with, someone who will get it.

An answer came one night many years later on a cruise ship heading north towards San Pedro. My companion and I walked to the stern of the boat, looking over the railing at the vast expanse of water, the broad wake of the ship, and the moon shining down on all of us.

I thought of the vast Pacific unfolding beneath us. The endless mysteries of the ocean with its strange creatures and wide currents. The limitless universe overhead, unknowable. I thought of the intricate patterns of evolution and life expanding all around us. So much more than we can ever possibly grasp. So much bigger and more amazing than we'll ever know.

And here we were, in the middle of all of it. Engaged in our own patterns and evolution and dance. And it came to me so simply: It's all taken care of. From the fish in the sea to the stars exploding overhead to the complex hive of people laughing and fornicating and gambling around us. It's all taken care of.

I don't know how. I don't know when. I don't know with whom. But I do believe that we are all flowing down the same river. And it is, indeed, taken care of.

The Day I Understood Little Red Convertibles

This is my dirty little secret. This is not for my husband or in-laws to read. This is not for anyone to read. This is my confessional.

It has to do with illicit fantasies and surges of unaccustomed energy. It has to do with outstripping one's own perceived limitations. It has to do with being 41, a mother of two, a professional with a regular office job. I pay the household bills, I wash the clothes, I take the dog to the vet. And I go through my life with hunched shoulders and low-grade headaches. My mouth is turning solidly into a disapproving smirk, like my mother's used to do when she felt beleaguered and tense, which was almost always.

It was in this bedraggled state that I was strong-armed into working on the end-of-the-year play at my boys' elementary school. I had accidentally mentioned to the drama teacher that I occasionally design lighting for theatre. Once she knew that, she would hear none of my excuses.

A couple of other parents had been commandeered by the play committee. One of them, Keith, was a grip by profession, working behind the scenes on movie shoots, building and rigging set pieces. I stole away from work one afternoon and met him at the Community Center to look over the stage and plan our strategies. My enthusiasm for the play began to grow. I went back to the office, sketched out a lighting plot and faxed it over to him.

After work a few days later, I went back over to the theatre. Keith and another dad had spent all day setting up lights and backdrops and foliage; they had worked miracles. They had rewired the stage and erected lighting trusses above and on either side of it. Strings of lights were hung all over, laced together with beefy orange extension cords.

Keith was working with manic inspiration, rocketing on and off the stage, climbing the ladders effortlessly. His energy was contagious. I pulled on my gloves and we proceeded to go completely insane.

We rigged pipes, we strung cable, we wired dimmers, we created magic. My 41-year-old body was neatly tricked into thinking it was 23 again. The presence of a strong, skillful guy inspired me to my own feats of agility and dexterity that truthfully should not have been attempted without written dispensation from my physician. The smell of stage dust on the cables and lighting instruments acted as pheromones, seducing me into thinking thoughts I hadn't had since working my way through college.

During my last few years as an undergrad, my main source of income had been from showing movies and doing stage work. Most of my friends, including my boyfriend, were backstage techies—running sound, designing lighting or building sets. I was working four jobs, taking four upper division literature classes and figured I'd never be this busy again in my life.

But somehow I found time to hang out with my beloved tech guy. I'd sit in the sound booth during local rock and roll shows, or I'd hang lights with him for a local theatre company. It was not an easy life, nor was it particularly healthy. But in retrospect that was one of those golden moments when nights were full of rock 'n' roll and Sunday mornings always involved sex, Bloody Marys, and long laughter-laced brunches.

For the occasion of my kids' school play—the night of the rigging, the next day at dress rehearsal, and the night of the performance—I was graced with a moment of time travel. I was allowed to do what everyone wants to do: revisit the past with the wisdom of the present.

I was like an Anne Rice vampire, feeling the life return to deadened limbs, the blood circulating through my fingers and muscles. Even though food tasted better than it had in years, I lost my appetite. I could feel my hair growing.

My steps were bouncy and I looked upon the world with a benevolent gaze. I found myself acting with patient sweetness to my children. I even managed to refrain (briefly) from nagging my husband.

There *were* probably other forces at work besides stage dust. By night my dreams were populated with images of glistening forearms, writhing muscular bodies, dark thrusting impulses. The physicality of the work plus the creative collaboration with Keith put me over the edge.

I was taken hostage by my hormones. They took control and I was powerless to do anything except submit to their extreme demands. I looked differently at every man walking on the planet. I was a sexual being and commanded my power with skill.

I was deranged. I was loopy. I was completely alive.

It was an insanely glorious week.

Everything changed. I was too amped to drive so I walked everywhere, my manic crazed energy propelling me mindlessly through the streets of Pasadena. I grinned and laughed more than I had in years. Inside this previously sedentary body was a 23-year-old, and that person was glorying in simply being *alive.*

But there was danger involved. The crazed hormones kept me awake at night, working on scenarios that would enable me to mainline this kind of juice forever. Now that they had gained ascendancy they were reluctant to let me go back.

They knew there was no future for them in paying bills and doing laundry. Oh no. They wanted me to make the leap, join the circus, shake the party up for good. Find a muscle man, they urged. You're a hot babe, they sang to me at night. You're not getting any younger, they whispered hot against my neck.

Now's the time.

Now or never.

Do it do it do it do it.

And I'd swoon as I played Tom Petty and the Heartbreakers, feeling the pulses of sound pounding through my groin.

The show was a terrific success, of course, with tears and applause and high fives and camera flashes. Kids staggered around in costume, waving to their folks in the audience and never knowing exactly when to get on or off the stage. Keith and I ran the lights and sound in tandem from our makeshift booth, working without a script or any idea of what would happen next. In two days we had developed a shorthand and an ease with each other. In two days we needed no words.

It couldn't last forever. That kind of high is impossible to sustain; as with all highs, the letdown was inevitable.

The school year has ended now, and summer has begun. The music and lights are starting to fade from my memory. I don't know if Keith and I will maintain a friendship for the next two weeks or the next two lifetimes. I don't know if we'll make it through the summer. Our kids have become fast friends throughout all this, which gives us an excuse to keep in contact. But I have no idea if he always lives his life with such abundant creativity and energy, or if I've just existed in a cave for so long that any glimpse of light is drunkenly blinding.

I know the sirens are still singing out there, but instead of lashing myself to the mast, I'm now leaning out towards the rocks, begging them to lure me to places that were so dangerous a few weeks ago. Now it's me humming a few bars so they'll remember the tune. The song is fading. I have taken out the Tom Petty CD; the radio is tuned back to NPR.

For a few magical nights I was granted an intoxicating illusion of youth, laced with the hindsight and nostalgia of age. The crushing responsibilities gave way to long-forgotten feelings of power and freedom and joy. The effect was poisonous and addictive.

I'm glad I had that, despite the aimless longing that's accompanied the emotional hangover. It reminded me of long-forgotten energies, gave me feelings I haven't felt in many years.

I don't know what it meant. I don't know where it will lead. But I do know one thing for sure: Next year, I'm going to volunteer for a lot more school activities.

Context Sensitivity

For the past several years one of my duties in the corporate world has been to write online Help documentation. This is the computer help system no one looks at before calling technical support, and the system that tech support always tells you that you should have read first. No one uses it because it usually is worthless. No one writes it well because it is the epitome of thankless tasks.

It's OK if you don't use Help. I don't use it much myself. I'm OK with that. I enjoy my work anyway.

One of my favorite forms of Help for PCs is the "What's This?" feature. This is deemed to be context-sensitive because it is "sensitive" to where you're at on the screen and gives you immediate information about the functionality you're currently using. When you activate this kind of Help, a little window pops up to explain what you're looking at. You then move on, a wiser person, with one less nagging question in your life.

The first time I wrote this type of Help system, I became oddly and spiritually addicted to it. I started wanting to click on everything in my life. I dreamed I was clicking on books, on my television set, on my sons. What's this? This is called a husband. He is the person who once made your knees weak with lust but who now throws out the trash. What's this? This is your car. It has 72,000 miles on it—may be time for a service. I was looking at life in a whole new way: what is the answer to this object's question? What's this? What's that? What's everything?

One night, while I was working on a particularly juicy Help system, my half-brother Carl calls up. He happens to be in town and we decide it'd be a good idea to take our 88-year-old dad to dinner. Carl and my dad have always had a strained relationship and it's not often the three of us get together. When we do, though, we actually have fun and swear we'll do it again soon. Then years go by.

We choose to eat at *Buca de Beppo*, one of those lively, crowded nouveau Italian places, filled with lusty sounds and aromas. I leave Jack, the still-uncivilized 2-year-old son, at home and bring 5-year-old Chris along for the date. All of us are looking forward to the meal—my dad most of all. We order antipasti, chicken saltimbocca, garlic bread, green beans. Carl and my dad are chatting up a storm; the meal promises to be delectable; Chris is charming the waitress and coloring on the placemat. Everything is going fine.

And then my dad starts yawning. Yawning bigger and bigger, in a weird, kind of compulsive way. Then he stops talking. Then he says he's very sleepy. And then he slumps forward and passes out, his head on the table.

Carl and I look at each other, stunned. Dad is still breathing, but he's drooling and possibly incontinent. Carl is seated inside in the booth, trapped by my dad. So I jump up to call 911.

I make my way through the restaurant, towards the front desk. The other diners suddenly look like Diane Arbus prints, braying with harsh, dissonant laughter. Waitresses are serving grotesque platters of food; everyone is oddly-shaped, their teeth too large for their mouths, their clothes cloying and uncomfortable.

While the paramedics are en route, the emergency operator keeps me on the line, asking me questions I can't possibly answer. Is he breathing? Can you get him on the floor? Try rolling him on his side. Well, I can't do any of these things from my current position, and I'm not sure I want to be back there looking at his motionless form anyway.

The paramedics burst into the restaurant, their bright bulky uniforms creating instant chaos. I trail behind, wanting it all to go away. We are such a *scene*. People look up and conversations suddenly hush as we walk by. Then they start up again with morbidly curious whispers after we pass.

I assume that he'll still be unconscious (or worse) when we get back to the table. Instead, Dad is sitting up, his face still a stomach-wrenching blue, eating saltimbocca with a kind of fierce determination.

He looks up at the paramedics, and then at me. He's pissed as hell at all the intrusion. One of the paramedics is a Nordic blond, the other is black with Rasta locks. They try to take his pulse and his blood pressure; he wants nothing to do with it and continues to eat. We coerce and cajole. Finally we get his vital signs; everything is okay. But he's still blue, and getting more belligerent by the minute.

The paramedics say he should go to the emergency room for further examination, but we all know that would entail a serious fight. We tell them we'll figure it out and will take him on our own. They have him sign a release. We all shake hands and then they leave.

Appetites (except for Dad's) have been seriously diminished. He's intent on picking up where we left off before those goddamn paramedics arrived. He still wants to make it an occasion (which undoubtedly it's been.) We watch him eat for a few minutes, then give up and tell him we're going home. We skip the emergency room; no matter how much we may be jeopardizing his life, we simply can't endure one more minute.

As we leave, Chris runs to hug the waitress whom he's decided he wants to marry. She has tears in her eyes.

After hugging Carl tightly good-bye and dropping off my dad at his apartment, I drive us back home. I am shaken to the core, painfully aware of the exquisitely tenuous connections between all of us. Chris falls asleep in the car. As I carry him in, I feel his sleepy, trusting weight and my heart breaks with the aching of it all.

I lay Chris down in his bed and pause to give Jack a good-night kiss. In sleep, Jack is beatific, an angel. Awake, Jack is Dr. Freud's poster child.

It's all about control for Jack. There are issues every hour. Sometimes it's diaper changing. Sometimes it's getting into the car seat. Sometimes it's food. Sometimes it's whether he can open the door by himself.

Everything is an issue to this two-year-old. Everything is a symbol of the basic problem: he is smart enough to know what he wants to do, and yet his physical prowess is not able to keep up with his desires. He is frustrated, violated by his own inept body, howls at the universe, rails at the people trying to help him.

Just like my dad.

They are at opposite ends of the spectrum, and their lives mirror each other perfectly these days. Jack is on the ascendancy of the learning curve. He is gaining skills, learning tricks, implementing his knowledge more every day. As his mind quickens and assimilates, he tries to make his body keep up. The lags are frustrating, but his future holds ever-greater competency and rewards.

My dad, sadly, is on the downhill side. His mind is failing at a slower rate than his body. He knows that both are no longer reliable, and his tirades at that injustice are full of rage and howling disbelief. He is losing his words as rapidly as Jack is gaining his. He is losing his balance as Jack learns to jump and coordinate.

Like Jack, he knows what he wants. Like Jack, he frequently fails at getting it. Like Jack, he feels that life is pitted against him. Like Jack, he is right.

I look at them and see my own voracious hunger towards autonomy. My struggle towards being physically independent, emotionally strong and psychologically whole has consumed most of my life.

All of us, when we're very young, go through rites of passage. At two, it's about taking command of our bodies, moving away from needing our mothers to survive.

At fifteen, we revisit the same themes, and our brains again outstrip our physical ability to cope. Young men want to drive fast cars, screw cute girls, have all the money in the world, and tell their parents to fuck off. But when you are a sophomore in high school you cannot get control over your facial oils, let alone be master of the universe. You rail. You listen to rock and roll. You drink. You try to survive the imbalance.

When I arrived at my twenties things began to calm down, but I was still racing to become the person I wanted to be. Thirties (perhaps falsely) started to give the illusion of balance. Then the forties, I'm finding, are taking any gains I thought I'd made and spinning everything right back into chaos again.

My brain is still working faster than my ability to keep pace. I still feel that hunger, that anger that I am not capable of doing everything I want. I smell the first whiff of the deterrent called Age. I refuse to believe that I am growing older. Yet I sit here tonight with a bad shoulder from a clumsy fall in martial arts, trying to persuade myself that it's a symbol of machismo and grit, rather than the possibility that my body is deteriorating faster than I can train it to respond.

The downhill slope comes at some point. The learning curve for my father is behind him. His escapades will eventually culminate in death; my son's adventures will hopefully lead him to a fuller knowledge and enjoyment of life.

What's this? I look at my son and my father and realize that with them, more than anywhere else these days, it's my job to be context-sensitive. To try to answer the questions of the world for them. What's this? An old man, defiant and scared, who can still laugh deeply and make me feel joy at his existence every time we speak. What's this? A small child, angry at the world, learning daily about who he is, where his boundaries are drawn, what the difference is between his life and mine.

And I point to myself.

What's this? A woman stuck at the fulcrum between two opposing forces. Someone who attempts to balance and meet others' desperately conflicting needs. Someone who tries to guess what problems they're having and, in answering their questions, attempts to solve some of her own.

Teach Your Children

When I was in high school, in the mid-1970's, I was idealistic and political. It was in the air. The upheavals of adolescence kept me reeling and I channeled it by being angry at everything and everyone. I hated the superficiality I saw around me and craved to be part of something important. My primary solace came from belonging to a group of intense young people who were striving to make the world a better place.

Not that I knew what that meant. To me the world would be a better place if I had a boyfriend. The world would be a better place if I could figure out some way to get along with my mother. The world would be a better place if I could have all the freedoms I longed for (with none of the responsibilities).

Truthfully, it all had very little to do with the war in Vietnam or the crumbling icons of Watergate. It even had fairly little to do with my primary target of local advocacy—fighting to maintain the new bussing mandates in my hometown to start integrating the district.

But those were the battles at hand, and I fought them with all the intensity I had. I went to every school board meeting. I knew the political stance of every city council member. I was making the world a better place and I didn't care whom I took down with me.

I had been looking forward to the summer of love for six years when I graduated from high school. It seemed to me that the flower children up in the Bay Area had it all figured out. They were self-actualized and free. They wore what they wanted to, made love with everyone and took wild drugs not just for the fun of it (oh no!) but with the far loftier goal of opening up their minds and spirits. What was going on was important, political, and relevant not only for the present but with great implications for the future. I perceived a glittering Oz on the horizon, just waiting for me to grow up fast enough to get my own keys to the Emerald City.

I graduated from high school early and got out of Southern California as quickly as I could. I was finally on the carousel, and the brass ring was within reach. Now I could begin making a difference—in my life and in the world.

Well. Things happened. I spent a year at U.C. Santa Cruz, subsidized by my mother, who was not happy about my own self-actualizing. She withdrew her money.

I decided I could make it on my own and headed up to Berkeley, working several jobs and then (far worse) not working at all. After being $1.35 away from living on the streets, I finally pleaded my way into a job as a pizza deliverer. Somehow I was able to leverage that enough to put myself through another year of school.

I was exactly where I wanted to be: in the Bay Area, in the middle of the revolution. Or what was left of it. At such close range, the revolution was rather seamy, actually. Most people were strung out on hard drugs. The streets were desperate and threatening, not liberating and intellectual. I had made it just in time for the hangover.

I fell in with a group of street musicians, old-timers in their early 20's. By day they panhandled, by night they crashed in abandoned houses. Their movements were informed by their need to avoid people: their alcoholic mothers, gang members with vendettas, drug dealers hunting for fall guys. They lived with blood-shot eyes and a bravado born of fear. They stashed .357 Magnums under the front seats of their beat-up cars.

The drug taking was intense and freaky. Forget expanding the mind—these people were deadening pain as fast as they could incur it. I lived in a state of fear and uncertainty. Broken bottles were aimed at my head. The smell of urine in the hallways greeted me in the morning when I'd wake up in another unknown place.

Time passed. I escaped the revolution. I found ways to survive physically. Eventually I found ways to survive emotionally. I lost my idealism. I couldn't remember ever believing in the political process. I focused, finally, on trying to live my life in as decent and honorable a way as possible. When decency and honor were out of the question, I settled for just getting by. It worked.

I ended up back in my hometown many years later. I had worked my way through two degrees and had acquired a husband and a house along the way. My journey had taken me full circle back to the place I had escaped so long before. Time passed more quickly. Before I knew exactly what had happened, I was a mom with two sons.

Let's be honest. If I saw myself today from where I was when I was 18, I'd call myself the ultimate sell-out. What am I doing, working an office job and running my sons back and forth to play dates? What happened to passion? What happened to writing socially meaningful prose and living on coffee and cigarettes and dying for your art? What am I doing here with *kids*?

Kids were always considered the ultimate bummer. How could you march on Washington if you were stuck at home making fish sticks every night? How could you keep up with the latest issue of *Mother Jones* while you bust your hump holding a day job just for the benefits? You may as well forget all ideas of ever having a life, or a creative career, or an intellectual discussion. And as far as changing the world went—well, let's face it: I gave up on that long ago, when I didn't have kids. How could I even consider the possibility now?

And yet there are parts of my life now that are oddly reminiscent of what I had back then.

One winter day I found myself riding with my girlfriend in her van. We were listening to a Grateful Dead CD and ogling cute guys as we sang along. It was a glorious day and the only thing that differentiated it from college days (besides the technology and the fact that the car was actually running) was the four young boys riding in the car behind us. We were off to the mountains to go sledding; the mood was high and the vibes were good.

And I realized I would never have left the inertial comfort of my living room to just see the snow if I didn't have kids. With them I'm granted the magic ability to revisit my own youth. One rainy afternoon, I introduced them to *Yellow Submarine* and marveled at the same hallucinogenic dance of color and song that had mesmerized me many years ago.

Periodically, my youngest son's pre-school holds a barn-raising day. All the families to get together and pool their collective talents to help paint bookshelves, plant flowers, repair easels. This year, as usual, I deemed myself too busy to actually spend any time *doing* something so I bought my way out of the commitment by purchasing some shelving for my son's classroom.

I bought the lumber, delivered it, and was driving out of the parking lot when I noticed something. Someone had brought a boom box and James Taylor was singing. Parents were working alongside teachers. Kids' voices filled the air, along with the sound of saws and occasional women's laughter.

I stopped. Struck.

This is where it went, I suddenly thought. This is where the revolution went. We are doing it here. The dream mutated far away from the original blueprint, but it is alive now. Here. With the kids.

In the process of all the drugs, all the marching, all the squalor and broken dreams, I had lost the image of what the goal was supposed to be. And now, surprisingly enough, it seemed as though some of those ideals may finally be within my reach.

Sure, I'm going to screw up. Sure, my kids are going to be in therapy for years, complaining about how their mother spent more time stressing about her lost youth than engaging in an old-fashioned game of Candyland. But maybe it will be OK. Maybe, collectively, we know a little bit more than we used to.

Raising children—either personally or as a society—is the ultimate political act. And not in the way I would've ever understood back in my college days. It's not about raising my own consciousness. It's not about indoctrinating new little voters so they will grow up to embrace my favorite partisan cause. It's way bigger, and way simpler than that.

By thoughtfully and intelligently nurturing the children I've been entrusted with, I can actually make a stab at the original end result. Even though I am flawed, haunted, and inconsistent, they give me a way to make the world a better place.

Raising children is about creating the future. In a tangible and irrefutable way. If we can proceed with a sense of reverence for all that truly means, maybe we can finally make that summer of love a reality after all.

Purple Flowers

O*ne of the first weekends* after the school show, Keith calls to suggest a hike. It is a hot, clear California summer day. "There's a waterfall up in the mountains just outside of town," he says. "Takes about thirty minutes to hike to." It is just right for two young kids and a couple of adults who need to continue a conversation.

Keith and his son, Jacob, show up around noon. Chris and I are ready and waiting on the front porch. Keith is wearing a gray tank top, blue shorts, mussed hair, and a new goatee. His tan makes him look like he carries summer with him all year round.

We clamber into his red Subaru and take off, heading north. He offers me some cherries. I give the boys bubble gum cigars.

We drive up Lake Avenue, the grade of the alluvial fan of the mountains causing us to climb steadily and smoothly until we reach the foothills. I open the sunroof and the blue sky blows above us like a magical ceiling. No smog. No clouds. Just blue, serene, and promising. The city falls away behind us.

As we curl up into the mountains, I can smell the hot oily chaparral of the San Gabriel Mountains baking in the hillsides.

"Hey, look! A hawk!" Jacob points out the driver's side windows.

Keith immediately pulls into a turnout so we can check it out firsthand. Scrambling out of the car, we run across the road and up a small rise overlooking a canyon.

Keith and Jacob immediately spot the hawk that we had seen. It is a red-tail, and soars back and forth above the ravine, looking intently downward. In short order, Keith scopes out a second hawk's perch. Chris and I spend far more time in front of computer monitors than on windswept hillsides, so we are incapable of picking out any detail in all that *nature*. Keith and Jacob patiently work their way through the landmarks until we can see the second bird, too.

The two red-tail hawks hunt in tandem. One perches on a tree on our side of the ravine; the other is situated on the other side. When one sees something, the other also lifts off. They soar through the warm air, soundlessly working together.

We watch them glide along the air currents, looking for food. I think how effortless their partnering seems to be. How simple their needs and how elegant their solution. If two work together to find food, each one singly works half as hard. I wonder if there is even the most remote possibility that a human marriage could ever work that way, and dismiss the thought immediately.

Silently, we walk back to the car and climb back in. The road twists down and around, winding into a deep canyon. Since the sighting of the hawks, the four of us are completely settled and quiet with each other. As if we had just experienced something holy.

Even at six, Jacob is sure-footed as a goat and totally at home in nature. Once out of the car, he immediately takes off up the path like a mad man. He treats established trails with disdain, always choosing the hardest, wettest and most dangerous way to get from A to Z. He can spot an odd or beautiful little bug from fifty yards away.

He falls into the stream almost immediately.

"Well, at least that's over with," Keith mutters to me as he pulls out a dry t-shirt from his backpack and throws it over at Jacob.

Jacob strips off his wet shirt, tosses it back to Keith, and treks on undaunted, leading the eager yet untrained Chris into the wilds of the San Gabriel Mountains.

Keith drapes the small wet Spiderman shirt over his broad shoulders. I feel some place deep inside me loosen up. I hadn't realized how tightly clenched it had become.

The boys soon outpace us as they throw rocks into the stream and scramble on the boulders. Keith's demeanor with Jacob is a mirror image of mine with Chris—hopelessly naked affection mixed with a thin veneer of impatience. Keith carries my backpack until my stubborn independence gets the better of me and I demand it back.

We talk fast, as if using a checklist to touch upon every standard subject. We start with the shared experience of the school show, and then segue to the kids and various teachers we know.

Without noticing the personal turn, we start talking about our respective college days, our careers. He can't imagine ever getting married again, which proves that he is, indeed, separated or divorced from Jacob's mom.

When I realize I find this last part very interesting, I stop myself for a moment. What am I *doing* here? I am at once so rattled and so profoundly comfortable I can't actually think straight. I have never cheated on my husband and I am not about to start. But this guy is fun, and I am having the best conversation I've had in a long time. I am surprised to notice how happy I feel.

The conversation zigs and zags along with the path. We come upon Chris who has been left behind by Jacob because he has a rock in his shoe. He is nearly in tears over the injustice, but once we shake the pebble out and retie the sneaker with an industrial-strength knot, he leaps up and dashes off to catch up with his new friend.

The canyon is deep and narrow, and filled with huge, violently thrown boulders. The path changes every year, depending on how severely the winter storms destroy the mountainsides above. We climb over logs and lesser grades of rocks. Tall trees make it shady, and cast dappled light over the stream. The path crosses the stream from one side to the other. We slosh through the water and breathe in the mountain air.

The kids are soaked by the time we get halfway up the canyon. They slide down wide flat rocks and get into 10-second fights that last until Jacob spots a lizard or a hummingbird and they race off to the Next Big Thing.

Meanwhile, the conversation has turned to the dichotomy between the East and West coast, what it's like to live in L.A., how it feels to be at this stage of life. We compare childhoods and our expectations of life.

The conversation is like filling in the blanks, brushing up on details that have somehow slipped our minds. You're going surfing in Costa Rica this summer? Oh yeah, of course you'd be doing that. How could I have forgotten?

As we walk, I spot a patch of purple wildflowers tucked into a mountain crevice and think I have never seen purple flowers like that ever before in my life. The thought unnerves me even more. When had I lost the idea of purple? When had I forgotten about wildflowers?

Somehow along the way the colors must have started leeching out of the palette of my life. And the only reason I know that had happened is because I am suddenly seeing them again.

After about 45 minutes we round the last corner of the trail and come to a very tall waterfall, carving out the mountain and coloring the rock green. In front of it is a shallow pool, about 15 feet wide.

Kids hold their pants legs up as they wade, while a smattering of older people sit on rocks, watching. A couple of women share a drink from a thermos bottle; toddlers throw little rocks into the pond; a couple of young guys wait for their friends to catch up. No one is speaking English.

"It's like walking into a strange niche in a third-world country," Keith says as we pause on the edge of the scene.

I nod. It *is* like being in a foreign country. In every way imaginable.

We hang out by the waterfall with the kids for a long time. In short order I find myself a part of the community of people sitting on rocks and doing nothing much else. I feel my pulse slowing down. The boys poke around in the rocky crevices of the canyon walls, finding weird critters that skitter away as soon as the boys' sticks muddy up the water.

By the time we turn to go home, I know I've found something. And lost something. I've lost my complacency for a monochromatic life. I don't know when the colors had started to fade. I hadn't noticed that at all.

But that was the day I saw the purple flowers. I started smelling the air I was breathing, feeling the mountain underneath my feet, was conscious of my leg muscles as I climbed over the rocks.

It was like how I felt the week of the school show, but simpler and deeper. It wasn't necessarily sexual, nor was it laced with lust. It was a sense of recognition, of coming home, back into the world.

Take Me to the River

O*ne promising spring* when I was in my early 40's, I found myself in Council Bluffs, Iowa researching a book I was writing. The night before I returned home I stayed up late, poring over grainy old photos and City Directory listings from 1848. Thunderstorms flashed through the skies outside my bay window. Between the growling of the storms and the beating of the rain I could hear the disconsolate whistles of trains moving east and west through town.

I had packed too much into the weekend and had run out of time. I was working on a story in which the Missouri River figured prominently. With a city girl's naiveté, I had assumed that the river would be obvious from every vantage point of the town that used to be the "jumping off" place to the frontier, the gateway to all points wild and unexplored. But the town had changed , and the river was nowhere in sight.

I woke up early, determined to find the Western Trails History Research Center before I left. It appeared to be a park and wildlife sanctuary, which I assumed was right on the shores of the river. I had a few more things to do but I could swing by on my way to the airport, see the river, and check out.

The morning ran late. Thirty minutes before I had to be at the airport, I careened into the Research Center parking lot. The river was nowhere in sight.

I ran into the center, thankfully empty, and skidded to a stop in front of three women at the bookstore counter. I babbled out my problem: "... research ... writing book ... plane to catch ... books to buy ... *must find river.*"

The women immediately picked up on my dilemma and were soon heatedly discussing how best I should handle it. "Well, if she walks fast she can make it there and back in 35 minutes." "No, maybe if she runs, she can get there in 15 minutes."

They turn to me and start peppering me with questions: "What kind of shape are you in?" "What terminal are you leaving from?" "It'll only take you twenty minutes to get to the airport if you take the shortcut that bypasses the construction. ..."

Then one woman says "Hey, you could use my bike!" All conversation stops. I look at her and say, rather stupidly, "*Huh*?" She says, "Use my bike. I'll go get it for you." So I kind of swallow and say "Gee, well, OK." So she brings me out her bike.

She gives me a few pointers about the gears (that I completely ignore) then walks me to a large levee that seems to have a path leading over it to the river. She points and gestures and shows me the way to go, but I'm too busy compiling a story about divine intervention in my mind to really pay attention. I figure, Hey, how hard can it be to find the Missouri River if you know which way is west? I thank her profusely, jump on, shoulder my pack, and start pedaling like crazy.

The paths are wide and all well traveled. There are several of them branching off to either follow or break away from a smallish pond. I take a path over the levee that flanks a gravel maintenance road. Ahead of me the path splits around the pond, winding through lush forests. There are no trail markers.

I take my best guess, heading to the right around the pond, but soon find my way blocked by a fence. I turn around and continue around the other side of the water.

The weather is warm and humid. All of my senses are heightened by the pressure of time and the feeling that I am all alone out here in the world, pushing inexorably towards an ultimate destination. As I speed past the dark green thickets, great flapping coveys of black birds with bright red or yellow markings flush out around me, beating their way up into the sky.

I'm completely lost. The landscape is unpopulated—just me and the bike and the path. And I'm pedaling along, going on pure instinct and adrenaline, hopefully taking the correct series of paths, when suddenly … there I am.

Right on the Missouri River. Flowing wide and huge before me.

I start to laugh and then I cry. I dismount and climb down the embankment.

Thanks to the loan of the bike, I have a few minutes to sit and soak it in. I look at a bridge spanning the river about a mile to the north and realize I am at the center of everything. At the center of my life, at the center of the country, at the center of the world. I think that being here makes *no* sense. And then, almost immediately, I answer myself, No, this is the first thing that's *ever* made sense.

I grab random rocks and branches, symbols of the moment. I scribble a few notes in my journal. Take a few snapshots. I hop onto the bike and speed back to the historical center. And then I proceed to buy about ten pounds of books and line up a book-signing for whenever my own is completed.

I make it to the plane on time, all items on my checklist nicely taken care of.

But that is not the end of the story.

I realized something about a month after I returned from Council Bluffs. I was back in "real life" and it was raining obstacles and frustration. I didn't know where

I was going and I was pissed that no one was making it easy for me and handing me bikes when I needed them. I realized that running around in so many different directions was probably just about the worst thing I could be doing with my time.

And then I was struck by a thought.

There had been no need for me to spend so much time getting to the river. There *had* been instructions. The woman had told me exactly what I needed to know. But I was so happy about being given the bike that I didn't hear her words.

Had I stopped marveling at the wonders of the universe for just 30 seconds and simply *listened* to what she was saying, I could've gotten to the river quite a bit faster. *The instructions had been given* along *with the bike.*

It wasn't about the bike. The bike was only a means to a much more important end. I was in such a red-hot hurry to jump on and get on with it, that I hadn't done the obvious. Instead of nodding stupidly and *acting* like I understood everything the woman was saying, I could have actually paid attention. All it would've taken was for me to shut up and just ... listen.

There are plenty of bikes and time enough to do what is necessary and right. There are rivers to discover when we least expect them. My goal is to stop the inner chattering long enough to actually *hear* where I'm supposed to go. But then I tell myself to relax a little bit. If I end up taking a detour or two, I think that's OK, too. The point is to enjoy the journey. Eventually we will all end up where we're headed anyway.

Cleveland Sage

Keith is in back watering the vegetable garden when Jack and I arrive. His house is in Highland Park. It's 100% old L.A. A mixed neighborhood, hilly streets, old clapboard homes, somewhat run down. His house is set back, facing out over the arroyo, part of the jumble of terraces and windows and lights that speckle the hillsides. On twilight summer evenings, driving along the meandering Pasadena Freeway, I have often passed them and wondered what goes on inside.

Behind the house, broken wooden steps lead down to the first of several terraces. The first terrace holds a small garden featuring a tent, hammock, and fishpond. The terrace below is where Keith has his vegetable garden and compost heap, replete with wild growing squashes and pumpkins from cast-off seeds. Jacob and Chris are on the lowest level, down by a lower street. That's where Keith has set up an archery range.

Jack and I pick our way down the uneven concrete steps, finding Keith in the vegetable garden. He shuts off the hose and plucks one ripe cherry tomato off the vine for each of us. It bursts like an explosion of summer in my mouth.

We stomp down a long series of public steps to the bottom of his neighbor's property. The hill is covered with brown prickly grass; the wall by the steps has been painted over many times as Keith wages his one-man war against graffiti.

Keith has attached a vinyl bull's-eye target on a bale of hay and the boys are practicing hitting it. Jacob is good, has a precise, smooth aim. Keith moves a huge stump over for me to sit on while he shoots a few arrows himself. He has strong arms and a perfect stance.

He works with the kids, adjusting Chris' hold on the bow. Chris fires off a couple of good shots and feels like a million bucks. Even two-year-old Jack gets a turn. Keith stands by him and positions his arms, helping him plant his legs. I shoot a couple, using Jacob's bow.

We hike back up the steps to the house. From the kitchen, through the hibiscus blossoms outside the window, I can see the street below and the Pasadena Freeway in the distance. A deck extends out the back door, with a rug and chairs, candles and seashells. A row of prisms are set just so, to catch the morning rays. Above the deck, Keith has rigged various sun-shading tarps anchored with ropes so he can move them back and forth depending on the direction of the sun. Raymond Chandler meets Ken Kesey.

Inside, the house is in a state of marvelous chaos. It's filled with collections of odd things: marbles and Christmas lights and hanging African beads and Swahili dolls. Lamps are draped with pieces of cloth and on the mantel there's a weird diorama made from some kind of air vent. There are bongo drums and tuning forks. Wet suits hang up against the wall, next to a surfboard.

The *People's History of the World* rests on the arm of a chair, and authors like Pynchon and Tolkien sit in the bookcases. I walk by the tables and look at boxes of buttons, bowls full of marbles, an old lead toy bank. There's a box with compartments marked 40, 25, 15, and 10 filled with little tokens of some sort.

It's like a giant puzzle and I'm hungry to understand all of it. What do all these clues add up to? The possibility of going through life without knowing what 40, 25, 15, and 10 means causes a swell of sadness and fear. I drink in the rich complexity of detail like a weary traveler surveying the first sight of a lush oasis.

When dusk falls he turns on his lights—drapes of chili pepper lights in the bathroom, dinosaur lights in Jacob's room, white and red lights on the pink hibiscus tree outside the kitchen, and white Christmas lights sparkling below in the garden.

The palm tree down on the first terrace is festooned with multi-colored bulbs. He says he strung those on a dare one night with friends while drinking tequila.

I wonder if it's visible from the freeway running like a river far below and vow to check for it next time I'm driving by. It will remind me that crazy freedom is still possible in this world.

Nothing is in very good shape. The furniture is all kind of raggedy and decrepit, but comfortable. If the whole place had been professionally art directed the contents of the room would look clean and squeaky and new. This stuff is jumbled up all over, but after awhile it is apparent there's a rhythm to it. Keith is like a jazz musician riffing with found instruments and objects.

He loads up a DVD of some music videos that he had worked on as a grip. The boys disappear. And then he cooks. Nothing fancy, just small frozen cheese pizzas. But he adorns ours with fresh tomatoes, arugula and Swiss chard from the garden, Kalamata olives and diced garlic.

I watch him chopping up the garlic and slicing the blood-red, fleshy tomatoes. He opens a bottle of merlot and pours it into some jam glasses with pictures of birds on them. (He decides I must have the Paradise Minor glass, with a white bird that, for some reason, seems to strike him as appropriate.) I keep shamelessly poking into every corner, asking personal questions, reading the spines of books, pulling it all in.

He plays a CD by friends of his, a group called *Calexico*. We pull the kids away from a game they're playing on the computer and sit around a wobbly table in the middle of the living room, drinking our wine and eating the pizza that has been transformed to a delectable treat.

After dinner the kids disappear, and we talk some more. Just grooving and talking. Listening and sipping some more wine from our jam glasses.

As we leave, he gives me a leafy little sprig of plant with an intoxicating smell, to make my car smell good. It's called Cleveland Sage. He gives Jack a little toy elephant to ease the transition into the car, which ends up being not embarrassingly painful. And then we take off. And I go home to my husband.

How *does* my husband feel about all this? He knows about this new friendship, of course. And he's fine with it, he says. He says he doesn't care if I cheat as long as I'm happy, because then he has a happier wife and his life is more pleasant. He says this more than once and I believe him because my soul deeply needs to believe him. I assume he means cheating physically, so I resolve not to cheat physically. I don't go into the fine print with him, and he doesn't demand it from me.

And it's not until many years later that I realize that his cavalier attitude was deeply hurtful in ways I'm still getting over. Maybe it masked his own disillusion with the marriage. Or maybe he never wanted fine print from me, because he never wanted to be held to the same standards. Or maybe he really did simply trust me implicitly. I never knew and never want to know.

I didn't cheat. But that didn't stop me from changing.

Just like the day of the hike, I felt I was seeing the world for the first time. And I didn't want—and was not willing—to stop.

I was happy, and relieved, and grateful for my husband's liberated attitude. I thought to myself, Yes, this surfer dude is cute, but he's almost certainly not a deal breaker for a stable marriage. A marriage that may be a bit annoying and in the doldrums, but a pretty stable marriage nonetheless.

This cute surfer dude was most certainly a life enhancement on the first order. A herald of the call to adventure. The question remained whether he was the adventure itself, or just its messenger.

Growing Pains

T*he fall my son Chris turned four* and I turned 40 was an apprehensive time for both of us.

A few months before his birthday, Chris started asking some pointed questions: What would happen if he had a birthday and nobody else did—would he be the only kid in his school to age? Was his dad going to get old? He was nervous that his baby brother was starting to talk. And, perhaps most puzzling of all, he became passionately interested in who was still wearing diapers.

This was odd. He had been in underwear for almost a year and seemed fine with it until he realized there were some kids who still wore diapers. It became an obsession. Chris started asking everyone about their underclothes—my friends, his friends, total strangers. It was as if he was separating the world into two groups of people: those who did, and those who didn't.

Shortly before the school year started, I took Chris camping with some old college friends who were also turning forty. All our kids were about the same age. We were "old" mothers, women who had theoretically exchanged physical stamina in child rearing for a satisfying and lucrative career. (In truth, we were nowhere near where we wanted to be professionally, and were so blinded by fatigue that we didn't even care any more.)

Chris and I shared a cabin with some friends and their little girl. She still wore pull-up diapers to bed and Chris desperately wanted to follow suit. He nagged until I agreed to let him borrow one of her pull-ups. He put the silly pink thing on happily. But then he couldn't sleep. It felt weird to him, which disturbed him. He still wanted to be like her ... but the pull-up suddenly felt oh so *wrong*.

Finally, when he realized our next-door neighbor (a fully matriculated four-year-old) wore underwear to bed, he was able to take the diaper off and "save it for later."

But the issue continued.

About a week after we came back from the camping trip he made a very unnerving pronouncement: He wasn't going to eat any more because then he wouldn't get bigger. When questioned, we pieced together his logic: If he didn't get bigger, he wouldn't have to have birthdays. If he didn't have birthdays he wouldn't get older. And if he didn't get older, he wouldn't die.

Whoaaaaa.

Where was he *getting* all this?

At that point, I seriously started questioning how much of my own anxiety was seeping out around my carefully maintained perimeters. I have to confess, I was terrified about entering my forties. I was facing career changes, life changes, things I thought I'd be done with a long time ago. I was supposed to have it all together by now—and I most certainly did not.

I had spent my twenties in college, flailing about, trying to start a career. I had spent my thirties creating a family. This felt like the last chance, the now-or-never decade. Aside from those pressures, all this talk about dying had me thinking about that, too.

At the same time, I marveled at how my son had tapped in to the whole dilemma. If we actually could stop growing, maybe we could keep ourselves in an immortal limbo and never have to face either the scariness of life or the blackness of death.

Aging holds out a bittersweet concoction of freedoms and responsibilities. Aging means, ultimately, dying. Every moment I either cherish or squander sends me one moment closer to the inevitable final reckoning. It's all part of the big picture.

I look at Chris with vast indulgent love. Such big concerns for such a little boy. Doesn't he know that being four is going to be magnificent? It is going to be the year he gets his first bicycle (gleaming red and still unknown to him out in the garage). It is going to be a year of finger-painting and building sandcastles and fighting over fire helmets. He wanted to wear diapers so that he would stay young and protected. He has no idea how much joy and wonder are in store for him.

His fears are calamitous to him, yet it is so obvious (to me) that the joys of growth are going to far outweigh the risks.

And then I have a startling thought: What *is* the difference between his fear and mine? Being four and being forty are terrifying new frontiers for both of us. Of course I believe my worries are profoundly justified, but then I wonder. What *am* I holding on to? What milestones have *I* reached that I still don't fully trust?

Chris' new bike gleams in the garage. Yet even if he saw it, he wouldn't know its promise of exhilaration and freedom as he doesn't yet know how to ride it. Maybe I have some shiny new marvels awaiting me in the garage of midlife. Maybe there are flights of fantasy and adventure that *I* will get to take that I can't yet even imagine.

I know I can't stop death. But I have an almost irresistible urge to try to assert control over it. Chris's idea was that if he stopped eating he would never grow old enough to die. As absurd as that is, isn't that something we all do on some level every day? We shut ourselves down in an effort to stop living so quickly, to stop fearing so intensely, to stop striving with such apparent futility.

If I were omniscient, I would know the answers to all that the future holds, both for Chris and myself. But perhaps that would take the fun out of it, like finding all our birthday presents before they're wrapped.

The trick, I think, is to see the outgrown safety devices for what they are, and to respect them for what they did for me in the past. Chris tried on the pink pull-ups and found them to be more cumbersome than comforting. Perhaps as I move forward I can also stop clinging to the things that used to help, but now hinder.

It will take tiny, continuous steps of faith, on both our parts. Chris and I will have to revisit, time and again, the hope that life will be gentler than our worst fears. We will have to be brave enough to nourish ourselves and grow. We will have to trust that learning to ride our shiny new bikes will be worth the tumbles and scrapes. And just as I know his journey will be so much more marvelous than he can ever conceive, so I have to trust that mine will be too.

It will take courage, for both of us, going forward. We will want to go back to our pull-ups and safety devices. We will have to be brave together, my son and I. And help each other along as we take our small steps forward. Maybe the little acts of bravery will foster trust that the world may be a good place in which to grow. And maybe those little acts of bravery will enable us to gather enough courage to face the larger, and still inevitable, picture.

George Fly

T*he phone rang one morning* as I was frantically trying to get the boys out the door for school. "Kathy," my dad said in his deep, wonderful, aging voice, "I've got the perfect birthday present for you."

"What is it?" I grabbed Jack's diaper bag and Chris's lunch.

"You'll have to come over and see it. Fifteen minutes."

This meant an hour and a half—a luxury of time that I simply couldn't afford.

"I'm sorry, Daddy." I looked around for Jack's shoes. "I don't have fifteen minutes."

"You don't have fifteen minutes." His voice suddenly dripped with sarcasm. "For a fabulous birthday present."

"Can you tell me what it is?" Both Chris and Jack were nearing the end of their first week at new schools. I had been juggling work with their transitions and my nerves were snapping with fatigue.

"No, I can't tell you what it is." His voice boomed with self-righteous indignation. "Forget it. Have a nice day."

He slammed down the phone. I slammed down mine. Lovely.

My father had just turned 88. It's not as though age was changing his personality much. He'd always been proud, bitter, quick to anger, and capable of a wickedly cutting humor. At one time these traits augmented his life as a creative and powerful businessman. Unfortunately, in later years they made him something of a habitual crank.

Despite this fact, I believe he was happier in old age than he'd ever been in his earlier, more prosperous life. He was more introspective and grateful for small things, even as he railed against systems and bureaucracies over which he'd never again have any control.

And his love for me was pure, extreme, effusive and unconditional. No matter what, there was a bond between us that ran metabolically deep. It was something we both knew and depended upon. When his affection turned into manipulative ownership, well, I tended to snap right back. I am, after all, his daughter.

I hashed over the call in my head as I hustled the boys out the door. There was no way I could have walked away from that one a winner. "Whose birthday is it anyway?" I muttered to myself, as I threw their backpacks and lunches into the trunk. "Don't do me any favors."

But I couldn't dwell on my irritation for long. Other anxieties were begging for my attention. Jack was having a terrible time adjusting to his new pre-school. It was a marvelous place, full of all the most advanced educational devices that caring teachers (and parents' money) could buy—from water trays and interactive play areas to tools that help develop fine-motor skills. But Jack, true to form, was going through his phase with the same force of will he brought to everything. T. Barry Brazelton could've written a textbook about him.

It was classic separation anxiety, and I'm not sure who was feeling more anxious. I had been staying at school trying to work it through with him, then wrenching myself away amid tears and pleas to stay. I didn't know whether the new environment was making him truly unhappy, or whether I was making the problem worse by sticking around. Whatever it was, my heart was breaking for him every day that week.

On a whim, I ran back into the house and grabbed a Curious George monkey Tom and I had bought in Boston on our first trip alone away from the kids. Jack had liked it for a while, but then it had been forgotten, like the rest of his stuffed animals. Maybe it would help him through the day. I gave George to Jack in his car seat, and felt that familiar working-mother spasm of guilt, sorrow and fear as I buckled up Chris, got in the car and drove down the street.

Between my concern about Jack and struggling to catch up at work, I forgot all about my father. I guess I hoped the whole situation would simply disappear. I was a fool. The phone call came that afternoon.

"Hello. This is Maria, at the Bombay Company." A store I never let myself go into because it is all too tempting. "Your father is here. He wants to open an account. He said you could help."

"May I please speak with him?" I asked evenly, trying to be as polite as possible.

I heard the phone transfer hands.

"Kathy?" He was thoroughly incensed at the world's injustices. "You need a jury to get service around here." I could feel the clerk cringe, and could only imagine how long he'd already been at her, slicing her with his aggrieved self-righteousness.

"What's going on?" I tried to sound innocent and open.

"What's going on?! I'll tell you what's going on. I want to buy you a birthday present and these crooks don't want to take my money!"

"You don't have any money," I said, attempting reason.

"It's a free country! I can open up an account, can't I? But these jokers won't let me do anything!"

"Can I please talk to the lady again, Daddy?"

I could feel his quivering rage as he handed the phone back to the clerk. The poor woman was at her wit's end. She had called her local headquarters. She had called Texas. She couldn't open an account for someone with no driver's license and no credit card (and no money, I thought to myself). Finally, I broke into her frustrated story and proposed I just pay for it myself.

"Just don't let him know I'm doing it, OK?"

She was more than willing to play along. I gave her my numbers and talked to him again.

You're wonderful, darling." His voice was once again deep and proud and relaxed. "I knew my big shot daughter could straighten things out."

"It's all fine now, Daddy," I said, amazed that I had pulled it off. "You think you can tell me what it is yet?"

"It's a globe, sweetie. It's beautiful."

My eyes welled up. However much I am engaged with my life and adore my children without qualification, there is always a place inside me itching for foreign breezes on my face. I am a broken-hearted traveler, lovesick for the world. Yet I am too cheap (or self-aware) to buy myself something as seductive as a globe. It was the perfect present. My ideas of sneaking it back to get the refund evaporated.

There is more to the story. It involves my father haggling with me over how he would get the globe and its stand to me, insisting he would take two bus rides to deliver it to my doorstep that night. I settled it by saying I would pick him and the globe up the next weekend and then bring him over to a party my friends were throwing for me. However, when I went to get him that Saturday, I found him bloodied and slightly disoriented after falling down in the street. We spent half of the party in urgent care, patching him up and investigating the cause of the spill. But those things came later, and although they are certainly part of this weird tapestry, the next installment occurred later that Thursday afternoon.

I left the office shortly after the phone call to pick up Jack. I found him taking a completely soaked Curious George and throwing it over a banister into a sand pit. Over and over. For the first time all week, he did not come running to me with relief and joy.

He was happy where he was.

And I was elated.

In the car he periodically threw the monkey down on the floor screaming, "George fly!" I'd swerve as I picked it up again and again. Then he'd squeeze George into the seat with him and say "Friend."

Suddenly my whole perspective changed. Jack was showering George with affection by immersing him in water, throwing him in sand, tossing him around the car, stuffing him into strange places. In doing so, Jack was able to express his love for this poor stuffed animal and make it through the day.

When it came to being loved, I knew exactly how George felt. My dad was doing much the same to me.

My father had a purpose these days, going into the mall to get his daughter a present, feeling like a big shot when they "approved" his credit. My birthday present wasn't a globe; it was a happy father, engaged in my life and determined to shower me with affection, no matter how much I had to suffer in the process. I had a father with determination and fight and love in his heart. A slightly crazy love, true—but love nonetheless

I don't have many stories about my father when I was a child. But one of them involves one of my own stuffed toys, a Raggedy Ann doll. During some mythical time when my parents were happy together, they were in Boston, staying at the Ritz. It was winter outside, possibly snowing. They were drinking cold martinis in frosty blue glasses. And upon the bed sat a new Raggedy Ann—a present they'd bought me, an infant only a few months old. Like the Curious George we gave Jack, it was perhaps given more to appease the givers' guilt than to soothe the recipient.

Today that Raggedy Ann sits on a shelf overlooking my sleeping boys. There is a patch on her left foot, allegedly sewn by my dad after I had dragged her around by the hand for many months, perhaps years. The buttons on her eyes are askew from repeated mendings, and her dress is faded from infinite washings. She is battered and worn, but sits on the shelf with a fragile ancient wisdom.

She has lots of company. Throughout my boys' first years, everyone gave them sweet, soft, stuffed animals, gifts to be loved and treasured. But only one or two ever ended up as a prized possession, carried around exclusively day and night, the object of almost unendurably obsessive love. The rest of them wound up on the top shelf, unnoticed and dusty.

I'm not sure anyone has a choice in where they will end up. The top shelf is serene, quiet, and grants a lot of time for peaceful contemplation of the life going on down below. But it's a life of detachment. You sit there and watch, while the favored toys get beat up, dragged around, eyes gouged out and dangling by strings.

George paid a price for being loved. Instead of gathering dust and looking down on the tumult below, he was soaked and grabbed and stuffed into tight corners.

But preceding every landing in the sand, there was a glorious improbable hurtle through space. That was the gift he received for being the object of Jack's exuberant affection: that moment of wild exultant freedom.

If we have the curious fortune to be chosen as a recipient of certain types of love, we can embrace the fact that the privilege will entail bumps and spills, sand and discomfort. We will get broken. We will need to be mended. When gifted with a crazy love we can only be thankful and try to enjoy the journey. When we are loved like that, the true present we receive is the gift of flight, on wings that are not our own.

The Berm

Keith, the kids and I settle in on the beach, picking a place right where the sand slopes down to meet the water. The boys run off to the water's edge and start throwing rocks into the waves. We dump the bags and set up the umbrella. We push the sand down to make a berm, a protection from any stray wave that may encroach. "The best thing at the beach is making a place for yourself," he says. We make a place for ourselves.

The boys dig their feet in the sand, wiggling their toes while the water rushes over their ankles and legs. They hold their arms out, keeping their balance. They are new best friends and have been inseparable for about three weeks. The logic of the universe revolves around their double planet. They yell to each other across the sand, their feet buried. His son, Jacob, is bronzed and taut. Chris is less tan, younger.

The boys build some tunnels through the berm. The tunnels serve to keep the berm intact, a sort of release valve for the water to go instead of eating away at the downhill slope. The boys soon tire of the tunnels and want to go on a hike up a bluff. "Hold the fort," Keith says, taking off after the boys.

I sit, my feet against the berm. I am here spontaneously. I have brought no books, no paper. I wear a borrowed hat. I watch the surfers hover out by a rock jutting up from the water. The waves roll the smooth stones down on the beach. I sit. A frantic person suddenly stilled.

The tunnels the boys built fill over and over. Their top arches collapse. The water begins to encroach on the walls of the berm. It is becoming obvious that some maintenance is in order.

I get up and start pushing sand against the walls to fortify them. The water licks away the sand. I place one of the round rocks against the downhill wall. The rock holds the sand in place nicely.

I have a plan now. I start putting rocks all along the front wall of the berm. There are now three distinct areas—the tunnels have expanded to be wide throughways between the two outer walls. I practice stacking the rocks in a way that will keep the defenses strong. I think of my stepfather, a stonemason. I love the feeling of building something strong, even though it collapses only slightly more slowly than I can erect it. I range farther away, picking out just the right kinds of rocks. The water still encroaches.

Just to be on the safe side, I build a second berm, uphill about three feet. Since the first berm is under steady siege, I want to be sure to protect our blankets and bags. I redouble my efforts on Berm #1. The wall is looking good. The reds and grays of the rocks blend together, forming a whole. I start building around the edges, to protect the steadily dwindling mound of sand. The berm is now almost entirely made of rock. I find a strand of bulbous yellow kelp and festoon one wall with it. I stand back for a moment, thinking how good it looks, thinking I'd like to take a picture of it just to remember. Then a wave comes and wipes it out in a fraction of a second.

I run up the sand and grab our things, moving them to higher ground. The second wave comes in and demolishes the second berm. In three minutes there is nothing left except scattered rocks and a limp line of kelp. I go back to my solitary lookout.

One day, a long time ago, I went to a beach up in Big Sur with some friends from Berkeley. We had done a very good job of annihilating our brain cells the night before and had started up again first thing that morning. We were fried.

We had hiked down to the beach, a magnificent sliver of sand wedged between huge pine-shrouded mountains and aquamarine waves crashing on the rocky cliffs. We had brought a jug of cheap Burgundy and several bottles of water.

I flopped on my stomach, contemplating the steady eradication of the mounds of sand, watching the grains slip off slowly and erratically in the soft ocean breeze. I did this for about five hours. My friends were also engrossed in the dissipation of reality, watching their own worlds disintegrate. Periodically, we'd crawl to the water or wine and try to drink something. Then we'd fall back on our faces, watching the world fall apart.

Sitting above the wet remains of the berm, I flatten out some sand and use a stick to write down words that filter through my head.

I am here with a man who is not my husband. We orbit around each other, vibrating with the same frequencies. We have a strange intimacy, taking care of each other's children. He washes my son's hair. I hold his son's hand. At night while I sleep he leaves offerings on my front porch of things grown in his garden—sweet corpulent tomatoes, fragrant sage, hot chiles. Within a very short time we have gotten into a groove, speaking a shorthand, knowing the same plan. I am utterly and completely relaxed.

I call my husband who is at a party. "I'm never coming back," I say. He repeats this to our friends and I can hear everyone laughing in the background. I laugh, too. Then I tell them I'm staying over to camp out with the kids.

That night I shuck fresh corn while Keith makes pasta. I have nothing to do except try to help and encourage the boys to eat their dinner. They are playing with flashlights and toys and want to go down to a gathering a few campsites away. There is a rumor of s'mores, an intoxicating lure for a five and six year old.

We eat our dinner while they play. We drink merlot out of blue plastic cups. Keith tells me a story. He was traveling in Italy, and talking to a group of locals about how his life was going to work out. He was going to move to L.A., work in the movies, and everything was going to be fine. One of the Italians looked at him. "How do you know this will work out this way?" the Italian asked. "It is such an American trait to be so sure of the outcome of a plan."

Keith goes back to the van for another bottle of wine and I make an attempt at cleaning up. When I turn around the boys are gone, presumably on the quest for sweets.

When he returns we go in search of the boys. We find the gathering site, and they are not there. We wander through the dark paths, looking around, getting a little worried. It is not possible, I think, that this scenario will turn bad. On the other hand, says the evil storyteller inside of me, this is exactly how it would work out. A day in paradise followed by a horrific discovery, loss, tragedy of some kind. No, I argue back, that's just a Hollywood cliché. If something feels good, maybe it can just be ... good.

As we look, we wonder if we should be mad, or strict, or relieved with the kids. "We'll know when we find them," I say. They may be scared enough that we won't have to cover our relief with false anger.

We find the boys. The Hollywood plot twist does not occur. They were trying to find us and got turned around. There is no need for warnings or anger. Their fear is enough. We walk back holding our respective sons' hands.

Edges. That's one of the words I write in the sand. Being on the cusp. The kids, on the edge of being too tough to admit fear, hold our hands. Yet they were still brave enough to wander out into the night by themselves. Their own desires and their comfort with each other sheltered them. They didn't notice they were alone until they were lost.

And us. Shifting boundaries, changing definitions, blurring distinctions.

In my thoughts of him, he acquires significant proportions. He is a life force dispensing sensual flavors, tapping out exotic rhythms, evoking long-forgotten emotions. Creator of succulent life. Lord of a fertile realm populated by skittering lizards, sensual seething yellow squashes, tangled marching vines. He is humanity and laughter and worry and concern. Washer of hair. Singer of songs.

We dance a dance of intimacy and reserve. The synchronicity of our thoughts is a given. I play with it, testing it. I think about infidelity, as though it hasn't happened yet. Technically, it has not. We don't touch. We don't say the words. I have no idea how he feels about me in return. We either know or we don't know.

I fixate on the possibility that the entire situation may have been generated solely by my sad, lonely heart. The dance could be one of mutual attraction, tempered by as much distance as needed to remain honorable. Or the dance could be a device of my own making, my spirit bursting free, choreographing the universe with some sort of new and wild life force of its own.

I am caught in a whirlpool of emotions. I feel life and joy and anguish wailing around me, tumbling behind my footsteps, cascading around me like a swirling force field. Like incoming waves crashing on a shore.

The accuracy of the situation does not in any way destroy its truth.

The edges change. The surfers ride on the incoming waves, finding harmony with forces bigger than themselves. Land-dwellers build walls and fortifications, resisting the surges and pull of the tides and waves.

How do we know the outcome of a plan? How can we fortify ourselves against every possible contingency? The nature of the world is to break down, to change. The hard lines crumble. The careful structures fail. Children grow up. Loyalties shift in an instant.

Surfers find their balance by acknowledging the power of the inevitable, and riding it with grace. In the same way, the act of building the berm was a joyful one. The berm stood at the boundary between two worlds. It was a false protection between the fragile shifting line between land and sea. There was pleasure in the construction of the fortification, no matter how doomed.

But when it was destroyed by the forces of nature, there was only one possible response. Move the blankets. Enjoy the changing tides.

Conversations

W*e are deep into a cold autumn* after a summer of sunlight and laughter. Things are falling apart. Tom and I are in counseling and by now it's pretty well accepted that we are laying the foundation for a new relationship rather than trying to fix the old one.

I started the conversation after the camping trip. I need to be happier, I said. I don't care if it's with you, or alone. I just need to be happier. After a few months with a trained professional who teaches us how to communicate with clarity and understanding, Tom clearly communicates that he doesn't understand me, and doesn't want to understand me.

We are still working in the same office. We have separate functions so we do not need to interact much.

There's still a lot between us that isn't destroyed. We are able to keep it together, mostly. One day we go outside the office building to talk.

It does not go well.

He is consumed with anger towards me. It's all coming out now. I should be happy about that, I guess. He thinks I'm full of shit. He thinks I'm terrible. He's angry and hurt and lashing out. It's so fucking bad.

I go back upstairs to work. Reamed. Destroyed. I *am* full of shit. I *did* do this. It's all my fault. It's terrible.

I call Keith. He has become my best friend. Never more; never less. Chris is playing with Jacob at his house and I have to figure out when I'm going to pick him up. I tell Keith things are not well. I don't know what I'm doing.

I hang up and endure the next twenty minutes, playing Solitaire on my computer. I endure a meeting, staring into space.

I leave. I go to Keith's house. Chris is inside hanging with Jacob. The house is lit up; twinkling lights on the bush by the front door. I go in. Chris starts to cry when he sees me because he doesn't want to leave. I tell him I can't handle him crying and say we'll stay for a while.

Keith takes a look at me. I am wrung out and blasted. He notices without comment and says "Hey, look what the kids did today." He pulls out the little boxes labeled 40, 25, 15, and 10. Then he brings out some Tupperware containers, each holding same-colored objects—buttons, rocks, bits of sea glass. They are also labeled, with smaller numbers. The blue things are worth five, the orange things are worth three. I watch, numbly, as Chris counts out two blue buttons, an orange seed pod, and two yellow paperclips and puts them in the box labeled 15. I watch and feel a queasy combination of love, sadness, loss. And hope. There are still good things in the world.

Keith says he'll cook dinner. He puts in a couple of the little pizzas. I pick up some poems a friend of his wrote. One of the poems is about what a boy wants: a father to play ball with him until after sunset, a God who will look at him with amusement and love.

I go outside and suddenly cannot stop crying. For some reason I had sons with a man who has ended the conversation with me. For some reason those sons have a mother who apparently wounded their father in ways that cannot be healed. For some reason this summer I woke up one morning and wanted to live my life more fully.

In so doing I managed to rob my sons of an intact family. I killed the possibility that they would escape unscathed by their parents' stupid dramas. They would grow up like me, with holes in their hearts, with conflicted loyalties, with double worlds. Then I wonder if, given us as parents, they ever would have been whole anyway. And then I cry some more.

I hold my face in my hands, sitting on the back rickety

steps of this house that has become my safe place. While this man who is not my husband, whom I have never kissed, whom I may never even touch, makes pizzas for our sons. I sob. For some reason this is happening. And I don't know why, even though I'm pretty sure I started it all.

It's one of the more merciful facts of life that even though you may feel like it, it's hard to cry forever. So eventually it ends and I stagger back inside. I ask Keith for some strong alcoholic beverage. He pulls out some wine. I shake my head, No. He finds a bottle of Jim Beam. I nod and he pours some in the jam jar glasses. I sit down on the kitchen floor and suck it up. Wrecked.

Finally, he asks if I want to go outside, and he holds out his big strong hand. I haul my weary body into a standing position and we go outside. The boys are eating. Our food can wait.

I tell him everything. I'm consumed with self-loathing and misery, all in a snarl inside. I'm consumed by pain and he listens. He talks about what happened with him and his ex-wife. And I mention a time he and I had gone to the museum with all three kids. He had offered to push Jack's stroller for me and that had felt like the most wonderful thing anyone had done for me for a long time. I tell him I will always be so very grateful to him for that one gesture.

We go down to his garden, out under the full moon, glasses in hand. We pick peppers and squash blossoms and sage by flashlight. We marvel at the squash plant that has now taken over everything. And then we take it back up to the house and he cooks it all up with some garlic and puts it on the pizza.

So many times I've found myself driving late at night—usually tired, alone, sad and at odds with something—looking at the lights behind the windows. Sometimes there is snow on the ground. Or the moon casts shiny steel shadows through the trees. But the lights are one of two kinds. Either they are a warm amber glow. Or they are flickering and blue.

I imagine the people inside. Maybe it's an old man, hunkered down, eating a bowl of soup. Or maybe it's a couple, all the other lights off as they entangle themselves on the sofa, engrossed in narrative and themselves. I don't kid myself that everyone is happy behind those windows. But in my imagination it's always quiet and somewhat peaceful. Life has stopped in there, while I am still going, the miles long ahead.

What does go on behind those windows? People are in the beginnings, middles and ends of their conversations with each other. Even people alone are having their conversations, with themselves, with dead people, with people they may not yet know. The beginnings of a conversation are usually fun. The world is opening up, filled with possibilities. Jokes are still funny. Skin tingles when it is accidentally touched.

The middles can be wonderful, or they can slowly suck

your soul dry. This is when it becomes clear whether the possibilities will continue expanding or whether you are drilling into a limited resource and will have to research alternative energy sources pretty damn soon.

Silence in the middle can be the rich loamy sort of silence, filled with the exchange of thoughts, affirmations, subtle warnings, gestures of love. Silence in the middle can also be stultifying, agonizing, pained. This is the silence that is only complicated more by sound. There is a silence in which both sets of gears are racing so fast that they are almost audible, as each person conducts their own internal dialog with the other, too disgusted or tired to find out what would actually be said if words were uttered. Worse, there is the silence of the deadening of both hearts, so that there are no words left, no thoughts left, no nothing left. Just a thick gauzy numbness and a desire to get to the next source of distraction.

The end of a conversation, though … I don't remember ever feeling the pain of an ended conversation before. Not this badly. The worst part in *Who's Afraid of Virginia Woolf?* is when George pulls the final cruelty and stops playing the game with Martha. It devastates her far worse than all the horrible words exchanged all evening. Not playing the game anymore is far worse than playing with venom and malice. Not playing the game is death. It's a silence of no conversation whatsoever. The silence of the grave.

Breaking New Ground

In the backyard of my new apartment I've carved out a small space for a garden. My backyard is smaller than a tent and I dug out some grass along the wall, giving myself a two-foot ribbon that gets just enough sun per day to grow things.

I tore out the grass, watching the way the root structures worked. Some balls of grass went subterranean; others sent out feelers every six inches or so, grabbing so hard into the ground that it felt like fingers clutching desperately to life.

I bought some Bumper Crop, the soil amendment that Keith used in his garden. It was filled with all sorts of fascinating ingredients such as bat guano and about a dozen other types of manure. I silently thanked all the bats that so freely gave of their excrement so that I could have this experience. I wondered how exactly this stuff was harvested, and then realized that there are people in the world who think about such things for a living and that they would know the process better than I would. And I was happy they existed.

After I dug out my patch and made the soil rich with several bags of fertilizer, I outlined it carefully with red bricks hauled over from another part of the yard.

I took myself to an upscale nursery and wandered around in an overloaded daze. How could I—a person who has lived on this planet for a good many years—how could I be so *completely* ignorant about all these *plants*? I didn't have a clue what this stuff was. And there were people walking around, picking through the pots, like this made total sense.

I finally realized that accepting my ignorance was the first step away from it. So I found a guy who didn't look totally spaced out and approached him. It's one thing to be stupid in front of someone who seems kind of with it—it's another thing to be a fool in front of someone who looks like he's been smoking his wares for twenty years, and spends the rest of his time eschewing red meat.

I got the confessions over with and went right to the things I knew: I wanted to plant something. In the ground. I couldn't tell him that all I wanted was an excuse to be outside, get my fingers dirty, think new thoughts and get used to being divorced, so I told him I wanted the plants I plant to have something useful coming out of them in some form or another. Like, maybe, vegetables. Or herbs.

"What's the exposure?" he asked. I hesitated, calculating the orientation of the nearest freeway.

"East," I answered, finally.

"How much sun do you get a day?"

That one was trickier. If I'd ever spent a full day in my yard I might know this, but I don't. I tried to triangulate the angle of the sun over the hedge and the height of the apartment wall behind the plot. Trigonometry, as I'd long suspected, was no help whatsoever in real life.

"Ah ... maybe five hours?" I eventually suggest, as though it was a question he could possibly answer.

He took pity on me as one would a homeless dog, and guided me gently around as he introduced me to an assortment of herbs and plants with magical names that would make Willy Wonka proud. We found soft fuzzy Lambs Ear and Feverfew, the miracle herb that was going to cure me of my migraines, and Borage and Chamomile. I went crazy over the pure existence of Chocolate Mint, which actually does taste like chocolate. And I loaded up on Indigo Sage and Mexican Sage and (of course) Cleveland Sage.

I gathered up probably twice as many plants as could fit in my tiny plot of newly-guano'd soil, but I figured, Hey, how big could these little things get, anyway? They were like kittens being given away in front of the supermarket—so small and sweet ... I couldn't give any one of them up. So I bought the lot.

I impregnated the soil with the new little plants, tenderly prizing apart their root balls and setting them in their places. Pushing the soil around the tops made me feel humble and maternal and omnipotent, all at the same time.

As I planted, I thought about my own perimeters. Just as I had lined my small plot of soil with bricks, I realized I needed to outline the places where I was going to grow my new thoughts and fragile feelings. Those places needed to be kept sacred.

Once the perimeter was outlined, I could build a fence around the whole thing. That metaphorical fence did not need be four feet thick and made of granite, but it did need to be clearly defined. My internal fence would not be built to trap me; instead it would serve to define the outline of my world, to myself and those around me.

Other people should be able to visit my internal garden, so I would put in a gate. That would be OK. But I would be in charge of the gate, and I would decide when it got too crowded or when it was time to just be quiet and nourish myself with the sun and the water and the movements of the planets.

And when that time came, I could usher out my guests and they could go back and tend to their own gardens. People could not come into my sanctuary and expect to live there, subsisting off my herbs and vegetables. They have their own plot of land to tend. Each person's inner life must be maintained or it will wither and die.

As I watched my plants grow up to be strong and hardy, I realized that much of this is pretty simple, as long as certain fundamental needs are met. My internal garden had turned rock-solid with drought and neglect. A dying garden, a famished soul, is the state of being internally impoverished. It is walking death.

It is easy to lose our soul when we let our garden wither from neglect, or become trampled on by careless feet. In *Harry Potter* the evil Dementors inflict the ultimate torture: the kiss of death that sucks the soul out of you. Beware: we raise our faces all too often to people or situations that result in a Dementor's kiss.

Our job—and it's not an easy one—is to know the extent of our garden and maintain it carefully. If we claim too much territory and keep ourselves busy and isolated in its vastness, we will lose our desire to venture out or receive visitors. And yet, if we hem ourselves in with a paucity of space, we will not be able to grow enough to nourish ourselves and will become restless and lose interest.

It is of course much harder to replenish our souls than it is to go to the local nursery and grab some more Bumper Crop. The paths to renewal are much less obvious than that. We are not allowed to stop and start again easily. If we don't know ourselves and tend ourselves then we lose ourselves.

On the other hand, after several periods of severe drought, maybe we become smart enough to learn some spiritual irrigation techniques such as yoga, meditation, hip hop—whatever nourishes and restores. Then we can more easily access the spiritual guano when we need to. Once the inner landscape is exhausted, it's damn hard to start over.

In the course of my life, I've met people who seem to be living a hardscrabble existence. They are impossible to penetrate. Words like "digging in" and "taking root" seem to not resonate. They seem to have closed themselves off and their garden has become dark and lifeless from overprotection or undernourishment.

I've also met people who have verdant rich foliage and juicy tropical fruits bursting from the seams of their personality. These people have a hard time containing all the thoughts and feelings and excitement they feel. This is the kind of person I want to be. I want to have all that.

At the same time, I want to be able to go inside my garden from time to time and shut the gate. I want to protect my growth, nurture it, and feed from it when I need to. I tend to invite too many people in at any given time, and it becomes overpopulated, hectic, noisy and depleted.

Tending that garden was the single loveliest part of my day. I'd sip my coffee or tea while standing outside my kitchen window, sprinkling the plants that grew fat and huge and unruly in front of my eyes. When they became crowded and threatened to suffocate each other, I cut them back, gathered large bunches of Chamomile and Feverfew and hung them on my walls to dry, so I could make tea in the winter.

Every morning, ritualistically, I nibbled on the Chocolate Mint. I crushed the leaves of the Cleveland Sage in my hands and felt that no perfume in the world could smell as richly sweet. The first water on the hot soil in the summer mornings was heady with ozone and life. I could breathe out there. I could start the long process of healing.

Drinking the tea from the medicinal herbs was not nearly as effective as the growing of the plants themselves. Standing there watering, with the morning sun on my back, I slowly and almost imperceptibly felt my neck and shoulders relax. My tight forehead began to unwind. My fortresses slowly started to send their guards out for coffee breaks, and then lunch hours ... and finally home to go rest for awhile.

End

The spring after the summer it all started, my relationship with Keith ended.

Not that it was ever a "Relationship." Not that it won't always be a friendship. But one day the magic intricacies we had together just vanished. He started getting cagey, started retreating, stopped calling.

In our conversations I suspected that he felt it was his fault my marriage disintegrated. He hated that thought and it would not dislodge itself despite my repeated statements that it wasn't about him. I was honest that I'd started feeling alive again because of our friendship. I was honest about that. And we both knew that nothing physical had ever happened. But still, he took his role as the catalyst very seriously and it gnawed at his soul.

I felt bad because suddenly the buoyant and life-enhancing friendship we had while I was married became cloying and burdensome (to him) now that I wasn't. I worried at night that I had misread everything. His new inexplicable busy-ness and half-truth evasions made me crazy. Was I taking things too hard because I was newly divorced and feeling raw? Or was he pulling away? And what had been my expectations anyway? Was I totally lying to myself that this was just a friendship and nothing more? And how could I ever answer that without ever having "That Talk" with him?

In the end, it didn't matter at all what the answers were. My feelings remained the same—hurt, disappointed, self-protective. Anger disappeared rapidly—he'd given me so much I could never sustain anger. But I was sad, yes, and highly disappointed.

So I retreated. I expanded my working circle of friends. I tended my garden. I tried to regroup.

The universe had been shot through with a different and wondrous light when Keith was part of the equation. The icons that had been bursting with resonance were now flat. I was afraid that the color would go out of the world, but it didn't.

I realized that now I had done the toughest thing imaginable, I couldn't stop and go back to complacency. I'd spoken unspeakable words and had paid a huge price. Going forward I could never disrespect that sacrifice, could not cheapen what I'd been through.

So I had to take back my heart, be my own soul proprietor. I needed to start the long journey towards creating my own light. I had a glimpse of what living the bursting-at-the-seams life was like, and I now understood I wasn't going to get any jumpstarts in living it. Keith was a conduit to the good stuff, and he had served his purpose.

I have an image of me charging, running out of a gate—wham!—like lightning. I see Keith and check my pace, waiting for him to catch up.

He stands there.

I jog around him, muscles primed, just ready to take off.

He stands there.

I desperately want him to run with me but he doesn't. Finally, he starts to respond by backing off, not meeting my glance.

So I take off again. Alone. And sad. But on the trajectory I must follow: my own path.

The Aphrodite Phase

I'd like to think that in every woman's life there's a point where she feels a perfect cocktail of sexual confidence coursing through her blood and out the tips of her hair. This cocktail would include self-awareness, self-respect, wisdom, grace and a great deal of compassion for the mortals who fall under her spell.

You can see it in young teens, of course—the Lolitas of the world, tan and lithe, laughing with their friends as they amuse themselves with the heads they turn. You can see it in some old women, if you look for a certain something in their walk or eyes. It's a knowingness. And a freedom.

I think women who fall under the spell of Aphrodite during mid-life are luckier than the ones who drink the divine juice earlier on. It's great payback for the years of high school agony, the wild 20's and the earnest 30's. The 40's seem to be the time to cut loose. The body is working better than ever (or can, if nurtured a bit), the brain is still sharp (except for that business of the perpetually misplaced keys), and the kids, hopefully, are old enough that they are no longer a source of total and constant fatigue.

The Aphrodite magic in midlife is delicious. It's flavored by an attitude of adventure and openness, freedom from fear and a willingness to abandon the checklist when it comes to choosing partners. Perhaps it's about finally coming up with the *right* checklist for figuring out the men to let into your life ... a checklist that takes in more factors than age, height, income and type of car.

I first noticed Aphrodite about a year after I moved to my apartment. She's a little annoying as a roommate but no one could say she's boring. She causes some chaos and doesn't really clean up after herself much, but generally she's pretty good company.

In some ways I'm sure I drive her crazy, too. But with her coaching I have become happy moving about the world. I do martial arts and yoga and ride my bike and walk. And despite the ongoing battle against metabolism and calories, I love inhabiting my body. I don't like making it feel bad with drinking alcohol, eating too much red meat, garbage foods or garbage thinking. After years of ridiculously clear object lessons, I'm learning to prefer feeling good to feeling bad. Duh.

Aphrodite has taught me that it's OK to have adventures—both in the bedroom and out in the world. To be free from constraints. To dump the self-consciousness. And even when I am perfectly satisfied with the current lover and the libido is purring in the corner contentedly, she'll still sometimes knock on the door inviting me out to prowl. That just goes with the territory.

Thanks to her, I seem to have access to a certain formula that the media pretends they have the secret recipe for. According to the movies and ads, the Aphrodite magic may be purchased in the cosmetics section, the lingerie department, by adding, subtracting or otherwise moving body mass around, by thinking good positive thoughts, by acquiring lofty indifference to men, by paying special attention to men, by being happy in one's skin, by exfoliating that skin, by exercising more, reading more, acquiring a hobby, cruising the net, cruising the bars, cruising bookstores ... the list goes on.

And I look at my life and I just laugh. I *totally* don't have a recipe. Everything in my life is being concocted from scratch, and it makes for a messy internal kitchen and quite a few trips to the garbage can. This Aphrodite gal is capricious and very funny and in no way can be contained by one set of rules. She just *is*. You invite her into your living room, or you don't.

Aphrodite introduced me to this thing called my female power. Men are cupcakes in the face of it. Aphrodite has taught me what it's like to think about sex 24/7, so my heart goes out to the other half of the species. I embrace them, collectively, with compassion and understanding for our mutual lusts. I love them as brothers and friends and comrades and fellow sexual adventurers.

Once Aphrodite settled in I had to learn, the hard way, how to juggle. Suddenly there were a lot of men in the picture and I had to figure out how to manage them. They certainly weren't all sexual partners, but there were quite a few of them. They were good men, too. Ranging from intelligent-to-brilliant, good looking to drop dead gorgeous, and really cool to really *really* cool. There have been young men, my-age men, successful men, struggling men, charming men, solitary men. I've hung out with men full of heart and soul, men with mischief in their eyes, men with aching longings, men who, with all respect, simply want to get their rocks off.

Where did they come from? And what did I do to deserve all this? (I mean that in all possible ways.)

Thanks to Aphrodite, I've found I have a weakness for the men who really love women. Womanizers are well-acquainted with my roommate and happily look past my boring clothing and the two kids to respond to the cheap-bait sass that comes out of my mouth. Womanizers love me, and I love them back. We twinkle at each other. We fall into each other's arms like long-lost soul mates. Womanizers totally get me.

I don't think there's anything wrong with this. I am kind of a man-izer myself. I collect men and cherish men and love them all. I am friends with (almost) every one of my ex-lovers. I sometimes joke that I'm so good as an ex that guys race to break up with me, just so we can get to the great friendship part afterwards.

Ever since Aphrodite moved in, I've had more fun than I ever imagined possible, and I've shed more tears than I ever thought I could. Being an Aphrodite acolyte is a wild ride and not for the faint of heart.

If you're lucky, she will knock on your door one day and change your life forever. Even if you keep her around for only a short time, her perfume will linger. So girlfriends, beware. You may wake up some morning and find her hanging out in your kitchen drinking coffee and pulling out her bag of tricks. I suggest you offer her the cream and sugar and prepare to move some furniture.

If it's too much, sure, you can kick her out. The death knell for Aphrodite sounds like the stuff that killed us in high school: self-doubt, self-consciousness, self-denial, self-deprecation. Once we start thinking about how ludicrous the whole thing is—how *old* we are, how *ridiculous*—the balloon deflates and we're left with what our nasty jealous little brains suspected was really going on all along: nothing.

So to all the women out there who know what I'm talking about, I'd like us to raise our collective champagne glasses and toast each other heartily.

Ride the wave gloriously.

Strut your stuff.

Walk through the world with a look in your eye that

will leave the recipient hot and bothered for days—and then take him … or don't.

Once Aphrodite's your friend, your only job is to listen, to learn and to make her laugh with pride.

She demands it.

And you deserve it.

The Words

I *loved his words.* His words didn't just move; they were break-dancers on the hot sidewalks of New York. They didn't just sing; they were street musicians in the tunnels of the Paris Metro. His words were gymnasts executing breathtaking routines; they spiked their dismounts with a precision that gave me the chills.

He loved my words back. Through some incredible chance, we found we each held a separate but incomplete dictionary, the words of one craving the words of the other. It was far beyond a sexual urgency. When our words got together they danced the tango.

Our words were instantly intoxicated by each other. The second day we exchanged thirty emails. We were up to a hundred a day within the first week.

Long before we even spoke, our words were making love to each other in long sensuous strokes, reveling in languid afternoons. They would take occasional breaks and then crawl back in for more. If language was heroin, our words would have been found six weeks later in some Hell's Kitchen backroom, intertwined, with the needles still stuck in their arms.

David, an old acquaintance, had somehow heard the news about my father's death. His own father, a long-time friend of my dad's, had died about a year earlier. David had written me a short email saying we could compare notes if I felt like it.

When he contacted me, I was going through an extremely difficult breakup with a married man. David was living in Seattle. When I had met him years before, he was living the good life and enjoying a witty and sophisticated marriage. The good life had continued; the marriage had not.

We started emailing and soon were voraciously consuming each other's words. We were both writers; it was a perfect fit. When I finally dared to call him, I was as nervous as a high-schooler. But his voice was good. And the words worked over the phone line, too. Better in fact, because we could get even more subtext out of each vowel and consonant. It was crazy. It was beyond good.

My heart was in complete upheaval. When we weren't

emailing and talking, I was shedding painful tears with my former lover. He had to stay with his wife and we both knew it. I hadn't even begun to process my father's death, or the breakup, and now there was this whole new thing.

David was about to go on a trip to Europe with his aunt. At the time, in the dark ages before Wi-Fi in every hotel room, this meant a complete break in our frenzied email accessibility. I was in agony. What would I do without the incessant flow of words? And now we were hooked on the telephone as well.

We were saved by an Internet cafe in Prague. One night he sat for hours while we wrote back and forth, the funny character sets translating his words into a funny gumbo—like letters cut out of a newspaper. I was seducing him with my words, while he described the world with his journalist's eyes, picking details for me like a lover picks flowers. By the time he emerged onto that old Slavic street on the other side of the world, we owned each other. Fully and completely.

I had an idea. A bright idea. I called him one night where he was staying, in some kind of castle on the Rhine, and told him the idea. I would fly out to New York to meet him on his way back. We would hang out together for about 20 hours. Then we'd both go back to our respective lives.

Oh, it was a great idea. He totally saw the beauty of the plan. It was so clear by this point that we were cut from the same cloth. He didn't think it was nuts. He didn't think it was excessive. He totally got it. It would be a Great Adventure.

Four days later and I'm in the airport terminal. Work is over for the week and my apartment is squared away. I've shed more tears over my dear former lover. I've masterfully continued to avoid dealing with my father's death. I've said good-bye to the kids and driven my sensible little sedan to the best-value airport parking lot. I have done everything completely properly, as befits someone who is about to take off to meet someone 3000 miles away, a man met once about 10 years earlier, and someone who will almost certainly become a lover within hours of our reuniting. None of this bothers me at all. The only thing that worries me is that in about 30 hours I'm going to be back in this terminal coming home again.

The red-eye is delayed. It's 3 a.m. and I am sitting against a wall by the boarding gate, bolstered by my new newsstand book and my newsstand water and wondering if I'll ever actually get going on this whacked-out adventure. With this delay I'm thinking, gosh, I'm going to be back before we even take off.

I finally leave and fly all night, getting into Newark around 11:30 in the morning. I ride the bus into the city, eyes scratchy with fatigue, skin oily and tired, my clothes already wretched on my body.

My perception of the Grand Adventure has shifted significantly. I can't even face what I am about to do—meet an almost complete stranger, stay in the same room with him, inevitably do the nasty, and then leave to get back home for work on Monday. Oh yeah, and I get to pay for the privilege. No, I can't even think about that. My only goal is to get to the hotel in one piece.

His flight is coming into JFK from Germany around 2:00 p.m. My image of having any time to myself to tool around the city visiting museums and pretending to have some integrity is rapidly being rearranged. By the time I get to the Port Authority and start walking out of pure nervous energy, I realize I'll get to the hotel at 22nd and Lexington just about the time David is landing. I will then have the entire time he's getting off the plane, going through customs, and getting to the hotel to sit and think about what a complete idiot I am.

I get to the hotel and am suddenly assailed by even more misgivings and fear. What exactly am I supposed to do? Do I ask the desk clerk for the key for the room reserved in his name? The Grammercy Park has been host to countless rock band rendezvous—am I just another flaky chick coming over to do the deed with the drummer? What am I supposed to do here, sit in the lobby for an hour or two … waiting? My God. I don't even know what he looks like.

I freeze inside. I'd never thought about this. I am notoriously bad at recognizing people's faces. My movie-going companions always have to tell me again (and again) who the bad guys are and who the good guys are. I just can't tell the difference. And here I am about to meet someone I've met, like, TWICE, whom I have somehow fallen in love with (yeah, right!! my inner voice screams. What the FUCK, man, were you THINKING ABOUT??) and I haven't a *clue* what he looks like.

Oh God. This is *bad*. I start looking at everyone who comes through the revolving doors with intense suspicion and fear. What about that one? What if that's him—do I have to fuck *him*? No WAY, I scream inside. What about him? No WAY, I scream again. NEVER! NO! Maybe. Oh YEAH, *that* one would be good. And so on and so forth. I am 100% panicking by now. I devise an escape plan. If someone comes in and I think it's him and he's totally repulsive, I'll duck into the women's room and stay there, like, forever. For an hour at least. I'll then screw up my courage and then BOLT from the fucking hotel. Then run back to the airport and boogie on outa town.

But how will I know? We'll have to make eye contact or something before I'll know it's him, and then I'll bolt into the bathroom. God, how tacky would *that* be? He'll know that I bolted because he looks repulsive. He'll know it's me and he'll recognize me first because he won't have that thing that prevents him from recognizing faces. He'll see me first, he'll look at me, and then I will run and fucking HIDE in the bathroom for an hour. And maybe have to crawl out the window. Won't that be sophisticated, Kathy? Won't that be completely COOL?

My cell phone rings.

I jump out of my skin, staring at the number. It's him.

"Hello?"

"You there?" His voice is the same. I relax the most tiniest little bit.

"Ah … yeah. I'm here."

"Great. Here's what you do. Go up to the room, order a bottle of red wine, two glasses, some water and some ice. I'm in the cab just leaving JFK."

"OK."

"The room's in my name. They'll give you the key."

"OK." I take a big breath. "I've gotta take a shower."

"Great. See ya in about forty five." And he hangs up.

I hang up. I'm in this now. I like the directions. I like the sound of the voice. It sounds … friendly. Not like an ax murderer at all. Or some big fat old perv. And I did meet him once, or twice, years ago. I would've remembered if he was totally gross … wouldn't I? Yeah, even though at the time I wasn't contemplating flying across country to share his room for ten or twelve hours, yeah, I would've noted if he was some repulsive creepozoid.

So I get up to the room. I quickly get out of my clothes and jump into the shower. The *worst* that could happen is that he gets there while I'm in the shower. That would be horrible. To just walk in and see me naked in the bright unforgiving light of day? No. Not good. And I can't order the wine before the shower because what if it comes while I'm still in the bathroom? So I race through a shower, trying to get myself to feel sexy and relaxed and failing completely.

I dry myself off, order the wine, and then fall into a total dilemma about what to wear. I have brought a sexy black dress and the usual jeans. The sexy black dress was for just this moment, the "first sighting" moment. But, God, isn't that too corny? Isn't he supposed to like me for who I am *first* and *then* discover what a sexy beast I am inside? That's the way I've always done it—I put a smoke screen of icky boring between me and the prey and then see if they're smart enough to want to see what's inside.

But this, let's face it, is a different situation. This guy, for starters, is kind of a grownup. I mean, he's actually older than I am. Which may be a first. And he's gone to the same good schools I went to. And he's lived all over the world. And he's funny. And I like him. And shit, I just flew across the entire country to be with him for 22 hours ... so who is kidding *whom* here?

I put on the black dress. And I sit by the window by the air conditioning unit. And I listen to the sounds of Manhattan fourteen floors below me. And I wait.

And wait.

And wait.

It seems like I'm waiting for hours.

My heart is punching me inside my chest. Then it stands still. Then it punches some more.

The ice melts and falls and I nearly jump out of my skin.

I put my head in my hands. I cannot take this. I was not born to take this. I was born to be a simple person.

To fold underwear at JCPenney's. To deliver pizza. I do not have the stomach for this kind of excitement.

And then, suddenly, he's in the room. In a blue blazer and short hair and horn rim glasses, carrying a roll-on suitcase.

I stand up.

I don't know this person.

I've always known this person.

He smiles.

He doesn't smile.

I walk towards him.

He drops the suitcase.

We meet in the middle of the room.

I lift my arms around his shoulders. He is my height, a bit taller. He is scary. He is not scary. He has blue eyes. We are both SO intense.

We look at each other as he puts his arms around my waist. Draw together. I smell his cheek, feel his skin against my cheek, and then we kiss.

We're good. We're very good.

We don't need words any more.

We emerge from the Grammercy Park Hotel in time for sunset. The sky is an extravagant canopy of pink and orange light as we look at it through the canyons of downtown. We look at the sunset and know it was made just for us.

On that and many subsequent weekends, we made New York our town. We saw *Kiss Me Kate* on Broadway. He proposed in the Algonquin. He proposed again on a marquee in Times Square. We had grits and chicken at Sylvia's up in Harlem. We spent one narcotic spring day in Central Park, watching performers and skaters and musicians calling up the harmony of the Gods, just for us.

We never got enough of New York. We drank it up and consumed it as greedily as we ravaged each other. On the day the World Trade Center fell, even though we had broken up months before, we called each other and cried with wordless bottomless grief. It was not only the buildings that were destroyed; it was our beloved city that was indelibly scarred. We had a ménage with that city, and when she was hurt it ripped at our hearts in a way no one but the other could understand.

We did other cities as well. We did DC, waking up before dawn and getting to the Vietnam Memorial as the sun came up. Then spent the day visiting the great statesmen, sitting at Lincoln's feet, standing in awe in the Library of Congress (the house of all the words!), and reading the Lord's Prayer to each other on the banks of the Potomac as the sun set. We got drunk in a Dupont Circle bistro as a summer thunderstorm pulled the ozone out of the sidewalks and forced the pedestrians to run laughing by us, huddling beneath their jackets and umbrellas.

We had a fight in Arizona and I surprised him in Colorado. We found ways to intersect that made every moment between meetings seem minute and meaningless. We transcended time and space. We were living on the pure essence of life; the void inside the atoms just didn't matter any more.

We weren't able to keep it together forever, like we promised, but the connection remains intact. This is an unfinished story.

Sometimes our words still sneak out at night to talk about old times. And sometimes, if the lighting is right and the mood is good, his will put on a Fred Astaire tux, and mine will slip into something very Ginger Rogers. His words will pull out a red rose and move out onto the dance floor. Mine will put on a perfume that smells like the gardens of Alexandria. And then together our words will dance to the old romantic melodies, and sigh about the slightly faded beauty of the world.

The Checklist

I've always said I didn't have a checklist, mainly because I've fallen for a wide variety of types—tall and short, dark and fair, rich and poor. I have always been open-minded about having my heart broken by just about anyone.

I realized I was wrong when I started talking to a man I met online. Dating after having children is more like dating in high school than dating in college. Unless it's incredible, you're pretty sure you won't end up marrying the guy, and you're not fighting the clock to find the right one to have children with.

It's a far different game than it was earlier on. The checklist is radically different, mainly because there doesn't need to be one anymore. I don't have to operate from a set of specific needs at this point in my life; the needs are more like wants, and the wants change constantly.

The guy online was looking for someone to have a little fling with. He was honest about the fact that he had a girlfriend. Any play outside the relationship was allegedly in the open and fine with both of them (the reality behind that claim was never extremely apparent). Refreshingly, this brought up some insights about what I was truly looking for. And how radically my checklist had changed.

I learned the nature of my questions because, in this situation, they were no longer necessary. There was no future, by definition. I was freed from worrying if he would be a fit stepfather. I didn't have to care how he paid his bills or whether his dysfunctional childhood would result in a true deal-breaker somewhere down the line.

If I asked him what he wanted to be when he grew up, it would be because I genuinely wanted to know, not because I secretly wanted to assess how broken his dreams were. I didn't have to feign interest in how his marriage broke up or what problems his kids were having in school. Hey, I didn't even have to worry if he was cheating on me because, by definition, he was.

I had to examine all my questions. What *do* I need here? Do I need a warm body next to me every night of the week? An extra set of hands to wash dishes and take out the garbage? Or do I just want someone to stomp out icky spiders?

How much help do I truly need in parenting my children? Would it be worth introducing a new personality into our beautiful little mix, just to get an extra driver to ferry to/from Little League?

I think our expectations as a society are completely out of whack when it comes to this issue. We are looking for the person who helps with the dishes *and* provides intellectual, emotional and psychological support. This person is also supposed to be infinitely (and consistently) understanding, compassionate, compelling, strong, sensitive, inventive, imaginative, sensual, physically fit and utterly seductive.

To top it off, this mythical partner of ours is also supposed to grow and evolve in his own right. At the same time he's supposed to allow and enable me (in a supportive and nurturing way, of course) to grow myself. The landscape of needs and abilities for both people are constantly changing from hour to hour, day to day, transition to transition.

No wonder we so rarely get it right.

And yet we cannot stop entangling ourselves. Our need to connect is as primitive and fundamental as our need to breathe. And, even though sometimes acts of loving do result in death, we cannot, will not and should not ever stop.

Thank God we're not completely cerebral creatures. The

arguments against a relationship ever working are so overwhelming that if we thought about them intellectually we'd never talk to anyone.

So we have to go elsewhere to explain why we do all this. And the place we have to go is, of course, the heart. That capricious part of us that listens to the other person's soul and has its own checklist.

What is the checklist of the heart?

I think it must have something to do with connection. Connection that operates on a deep subconscious level. Connection composed of an inexplicable mixture of smell, hope, memory and pure animal instinct. Connection that depends on a liberal, unflagging belief in possibility. Connection that continues and deepens and does not fray like an old rope when things start twisting and turning.

Lessons learned from past experience have nothing to do with the checklist of the heart. Nor does appearance, financial standing, marital status (unfortunately) or any other thing we typically consider when assessing a potential mate.

Connection is what the heart is all about. Without it, the other checklists are meaningless. You can have wealth, stability, companionship and everything else. But without the connection it all falls apart.

A relationship without connection is far worse than just being quiet and alone. A good solitude is like warm soup on a rainy night. A good solitude is when you're connected to your own soul and don't need another's to complete you.

Solitude is different from loneliness. Loneliness is when you're disconnected from yourself. And loneliness in its worst form comes when you have another heartbeat next to you in the dark—with a broken connection.

Connection ends up being only one true item on the checklist, and it doesn't matter if we're looking for a relationship with another person, or just the ability to have a quiet night alone with our thoughts. The checklist of the world is useful, but the checklist of the heart is essential.

Dances with Co-Workers

This is a story about the Office Womanizer. Every office has one. They are usually good people who capitalize on the long hours and close working conditions to augment their social lives. I get that. I do that, too.

During the Internet "bubble" of the 90's I found myself going from job to job as various companies that paid higher in stock options than salary went systematically belly-up. As a technical writer, it wasn't hard to find work, but it did get wearisome to be moving around so much.

One of the downsides (or upsides) of working in a male-dominated industry and putting in a lot of hours was that I was able to be friends with a lot of my co-workers. And, usually, better than friends with one person in particular.

The subject of this particular story had made the rounds before I showed up on the scene. I knew immediately upon seeing him that he was the one in the team that was put in my path to make me crazy. I saw him from behind and, even though I don't usually lust after bodies so quickly, his I did. Immediately.

I figured he was so cute he had to be gay. Turns out he wasn't.

I figured he had to be married. Nope.

I figured he had to have a long-term girlfriend. Naw. Single and looking.

I figured, last ditch, that he had to be young and callow and know nothing about life. Turns out he had been married, was divorced, had two young daughters, and they all lived comfortably far away in Florida.

Well, I thought, at least we know who in *this* office is going to cause all the trouble.

I watched him for several months. It was a small team so we had a few interactions, but mostly I watched. He was a flirt but seemed sincerely nice, and there was a constant stream of women in and out of his office. The fact they were all either married, engaged or had boyfriends only indicated to me that he was a good friend (and all the more available to me). (Note the inversely proportional lust-to-common sense ratio here.)

As I got to know him, he became more of a friend. I refrained from being one of the number-takers at the office door but we started doing things after work and kept a running flirtation going by email. I kept my radar up and fantasized lazily while I wrote user manuals and online help.

I figured he was so busy he'd want nothing to do with me. I was wrong about that, too. Apparently I was next on his list.

As our friendship deepened and flirtation intensified, I learned more about what he was up to with other people in the office. None of it was good. A screaming light was coming down the train tracks right at me and a bright red sign flashed DANGER, but I figured I was fine. I'd played the game a time or two myself, after all.

The six most dangerous words in the English language are "This time it will be different." I paid no attention to the warning signals. I stupidly introduced him to my kids; they loved him and he dug them. I was getting emotionally involved. From everything I could tell, he was enjoying it, too. But after it started getting pretty regular, I felt a shift in his demeanor. A pulling back.

At brunch one Sunday, I asked him what was going on. Well, there was a problem. His mind had kicked in and was saying that since I was too old to have a child, we obviously couldn't get married and therefore shouldn't be involved. Before I could even start sputtering in protest ("Child? What *child*? And old? I'm not *that* old!") he was already continuing: He was fine when we were together, but when we were apart his brain was working overtime. And it wasn't looking so good. (He forgot to mention that someone he'd been flirting with from another branch of the office was about to come into town for a business trip.)

We continued this conversation through brunch and then took a long walk. As we walked, we heard the cries of the wild parrots that fly around South Pasadena. One story I've heard is that their progenitors had escaped from the Arboretum at some point and now they fly in large noisy groups, settling in trees screaming raucously at each other. They are green glorious refugees from captivity.

We stopped under a magnolia tree, taking a break from the awful conversation to look for the parrots amongst the big waxy green leaves. We craned our necks and pointed the green birds out to each other, temporarily granted an emotional reprieve. We were as amazed by their presence as explorers coming upon an uncharted river.

Walking away, I said "Listen to me. We don't know how all this will play out. How can you take something that is happening now and junk it because of what may or may not happen later? The here and now should be respected. *This* is what it's all about. Finding wild parrots with another person."

"Yeah," he said. "But you can do that with a friend. You don't need a lover to do that with."

And I said, "No. With a lover, the leaves become more than leaves. They become nesting places for wild things. With a lover, the common is transformed and the exotic is revealed." I took a deep breath and tried to explain it a different way. "A lover has a sense of discovery attached. You walk away holding hands. You go back home and make love all afternoon. And with a lover you fall into a gauzy afterglow, and hear the cries of things still undiscovered in your dreams."

He got together with the visiting co-worker the next week. Maybe the magic of discovery for him was always embodied in the next new person, the raucous freedom found in a brilliant new conquest.

Whatever it was, it changed. We got together sporadically (after she left town) but of course it wasn't the same. I'd gotten my common sense back. And maybe he actually believed his own twisted logic. Whatever it was, he was drawn into himself. The free open landscapes within him were closed off to me, only open to the next person in line.

One night after one of our collisions I woke up at his house while he was still asleep. I realized the conversation was impossible to continue. And I would be stupid to stay.

I drove back home through Griffith Park, weaving slightly on the deserted road. Many years before, I had biked this path every day getting over another painful affair. My bike had been new then, and I named it Healing Light.

On this path I had cried and sweated and, eventually, laughed as I pedaled away my pain. Finding myself on it again that sad spent night, I knew I'd ended up there for a reason. It would be all right. Unfortunately, I knew all too well how to nurse a broken heart.

I sighed and headed home, wanting only to crawl into my big safe lonely bed. I curled up into a ball and fell into an exhausted sleep, knowing I'd have to go into work the next day and every day thereafter, pretending the latest dance never happened.

Love Before First Sight

When *I decided that dancing* with co-workers was ill-fated, I posted a profile on Nerve.com. Browsing the profiles there was more exciting than a candy shop to a kid. The writers all come off as cute, smart and sexy. They read books by authors I know I should know about. They listen to music whose titles I've only heard in passing on *Morning Becomes Eclectic*, and they sound like they actually *know* what they're talking about. The literate, jazzy conversation going on at Nerve evokes images of sultry nighttime assignations, seduction scenes on leather sofas, plate glass views of the city sprawled out like a well-sated courtesan many floors below.

Part of the Nerve.com profile is a fill-in-the-blanks

section: "_____ is sexy; _____ is sexier." So much for me and my degrees and my articulate brilliance—the best I could think of was along the lines of "Denim is sexy; satin is sexier." Garbage. But these other people would think of gorgeous things to write. I started dating one guy on the basis of his answer to this section alone: "C major is sexy; D# minor is sexier." Exquisite.

Another section asks who the profiler is looking for. My favorite there was from a young man who said he was looking for someone who will understand that he's "already mad at her for them not having met sooner." I was all over that one, too.

The Nerve site was scrumptious, titillating, mesmerizing, heady. All these wonderful men just offering themselves! To *me*! Best of all, the dance of seduction was conducted in *writing*. Nerve was my playground. I went in, broke hearts and took no prisoners—all without ever making actual eye contact with anyone. I enjoyed dozens of roller coaster rides, engaged in several bouts of heavy breathing (in various media), and it was ... sort of ... great.

Sort of.

A friend I met there said it best. It's as easy as ordering a pizza ... and ultimately just about as satisfying.

In the workplace, or in other situations where you actually get to know someone before asking about their favorite position(s), there's a base assumption of friendship first. Then, sometimes despite yourself, sparks start to fly. It's usually inappropriate, it's going to be messy, and there are lots of reasons it shouldn't happen. So when it does, it's because it's been significant enough to break down a series of obstacles. And when it ends, because you've been friends first, it is easier to be friends afterwards.

When you hook up with someone from online personals, however, there is an explicit agenda to get to the sparks part *fast*. Friendship, if it happens, is a by-product. It's very much like a job interview, where you qualify your candidate and assess whether he/she meets your needs for the job. It's fun and light and sexy, but underneath is a cold calculator keeping the score tallied up. And since it's entered into in that manner, it's usually ended in a similar manner. Sorry, bub, you're outa here. Next!

On the other hand, having an obvious agenda up front has its advantages. Despite the clinical aspects of the screening process, at least you know (or hope) the other person is available and open to progressing to a relationship. That's a big piece of information and it's good to have. Much better than getting to the sparks part with married co-workers.

The biggest problem, I think, comes with the sheer number of applicants. The value of an individual person is diminished because there is an endless supply to choose from. It's a menu system of picking a mate, and the menu is virtually endless. It makes it very easy to become a picky eater. Tonight, I think, I'll try someone with an academic bent, on the tallish side, but not too heavy. I'll take someone who is witty and high on self-irony but easy-going in the commitment department.

That doesn't work, so tomorrow I decide to ease up on the college degrees and go straight for artistic passion. Artists too weird? Let's just find some young cutie for tonight's pleasure. And if it doesn't work out, fuck 'im. He obviously was intimidated by my superior smarts.

These personals get very impersonal. And, of course, I've put myself on the menu myself. If the gentleman's taste is for someone with bigger breasts, spikier hair, fewer kids, or not as many summers behind them, then I'm out on the trash heap with the rest of my own rejects. Is there much sense of remorse? Not after awhile. There can't be. It's all part of the weeding-out process. And when you're at the wrong end of the cut, well, you suck it up and keep going. There wasn't enough time to get to know the other person anyway, so you can't even see the exact outline of the void when he disappears for good.

Sometimes you get traction. Sometimes very incredible traction. With one person I met, our email went exponential over the course of about four days. When they hit 115 messages in one day I realized we may have found the beginnings of something.

We were both writers, so the exchange was conducted in our natural habitat. It didn't seem strange at all when after a few weeks we were each exhibiting symptoms that felt a lot like "love." We had never met. We lived in different parts of the country. We only spoke occasionally. But in our different spheres we were walking, talking, thinking and acting just like two people who were in love.

People falling in love at a bar is not a problem; but

people falling in love through writing seems to be. For my friend and me, the first massive exchange was pure internal soul-pouring. We were starting a relationship in the place where most full intimacy ends—with an intricately detailed road map of the other person's deepest thoughts, feelings, belief structures, personal history, fantasies, dreams, disappointments and desires.

He and I already knew a lot before we even heard each other's voices for the first time. And, thanks to the efficiency of Amazon.com, we could exchange books and music. The amount of information we received about the other person was augmented in discrete packages, sense by sense.

Email provides an intimacy factor that is basically unparalleled in any other form of current communication. Even more than online chatting, email gives a way for each party to collect his or her thoughts, with relative safety, and express them in the best way possible.

Some people fear that the information being conveyed is not to be trusted. I wholeheartedly disagree. Far more information is conveyed through email than is evidenced by the strict linear words. Do they care enough about the language to capitalize their proper nouns? Are they sloppy and lazy in their emotions, resorting to the hideous smiley "emoticons" to indicate when they're being ha ha funny? How good was their schooling (as shown by their spelling and sentence structure)? How much do they *care*?

When do they write and what do they write about? Are they bored at their job and use company time to peruse the personals? Or do they wait until their girlfriend goes to sleep to hit on you for a while? What's their energy like? What they love is what they talk about—is it them, their dreams, their bitch ex, their desires … you? And what *don't* they talk about? What are they avoiding in their lives?

Information that builds upon itself slowly creates a far more accurate picture than most people care to show in their first social meeting. A crafty detective can sift through a collection of email and find out a lot more than is depicted in the person's profile.

Don't get me wrong. Physical information is very important. Absolutely crucial. And I really like being in the same time zone as the person I'm "seeing." But first impressions based solely on the physical aspects of a person can send hormones and emotions sliding down a very slippery slope indeed. How much information does it really take to (as a friend of my delicately puts it) "close the deal?" Two hours over a beer and a few furtive assessments of relevant body parts … many deals have been closed without much more information than that.

The other day I had lunch with an engineer I'm working with. He's Muslim, from the Middle East, and one of the happiest people I've ever met. We started talking about how he met his wife. He grinned and said, well, in his culture, you don't date. You just decide to get married and pick someone. He and his wife-to-be sat in her living room every weekend for a month and discussed "business." How were they going to treat each other? How should they resolve differences? What do they do if something unforeseen happens? Who they are, what they're like, how that might work (or not work) with the other person. After a month they decided to get married. Then, after two ceremonies over the course of about a year, they were finally able to live together as man and wife. "I didn't love her when we started, it wasn't like that at all," he said with a happy smile. "But I love her now, and she loves me."

I suddenly realized that what he had described was precisely backwards from what we sophisticated, hip, all-knowing Americans do. Discussing how to conduct business usually doesn't take place until we're sitting in the divorce counselor's office and trying to figure out what went wrong. In our culture, we consummate first, love second, live together, get married, and then try to work it all out. I asked my friend how many people were truly happy with his kind of situation. "About 70%," he said, matter-of-factly. "Sure, if someone turns out to be an asshole, you can change it. But you know what you're getting into. If you don't want to get into it, you just don't."

People in the old days—like before telephones—used to do this thing called writing letters. Letters are expressions of the soul, and were honored as such. Courtships were based on letter-writing. People fell in love writing letters. They took time to write and time to be exchanged. The elements of intimacy were concrete and profound. They were respected as viable reasons upon which to build relationships and even love.

Here in the electronic age we again have the potential for love-before-first-sight. Is it revolutionary? Is it detrimental? Or is it somewhat old-fashioned? Maybe it's possible that it will ease the way back into a more elaborate courting ritual that depends more on knowledge and understanding and less on the quick sell. I hope so. The power of this kind of interaction is not to be dismissed, and it's not to be feared. It's a movement back to a perhaps more proper order of things. Where knowledge comes before data. Where thought comes before action.

The Napalm Incident

"S*o, why do you shave?*" asked Antonia The Skin Goddess as she prepared to rip another hunk of hair off of my pubis.

The question takes me aback. What does she mean, *why*? Sure, it's painful, stupid, infantilizing and a servile act that completely plays into an immature male fantasy. Sure, it's nearly impossible to get all the hair off, causing hours of fussing and various expenditures of money on products that invariably gather dust on the shelf after one use. Sure, it makes my labial folds look like a combination of my grandmother and a little girl, both highly disturbing images.

"Ah," I stall for time, between clenched teeth. "Why do I shave?"

"Yeah," she says, daubing on more glue and ripping another chunk off. "Why do you shave all of it?"

Oh. *All* of it. That's an even trickier question. I shave *all* of it because, well, I didn't actually have much of a choice in the matter. The first time it came off, I wasn't actually the one who did it. So I have just kept going along trying for the completely bald, clean, smooth look. We'll get to how close I ever got to that ideal in a second. But, in theory, we were going for clean and smooth, well ... because.

I wondered if she was asking because she wanted to know, in a kinky fashion, what *I* actually got out of being totally shaven. Well, truthfully, it feels *great*. Great. Great in a sexy way. Great in a way that feels good in jeans, in hose, and skin to skin. A friend once told me about how he'd shave his head and then sleep on a satin pillowcase. It was the ultimate sensuality, he said. And this was, I imagined, very similar. And the smoother I could get it, the better it felt. To me. All infantalizing and grandmotherly labial folds aside. It just feels great and I love it.

But why the question about why I shave *all* of it? I *hated* that little fucking tuft right over the top of the crack. No matter what I did, no matter how hard I stretched the skin or scraped the razor, no matter how I positioned my legs or what shaving cream, gel, soap or temperature of water I tried—I just could *not* get that tuft completely gone.

I went berserk over that tuft. I got a little obsessive compulsive about it: once it was gone, somehow it had to stay gone. And I just could not keep it off. It's like there is a remnant of wild boar DNA hidden inside of me that is tenaciously determined to show itself right *there.*

The hair there isn't just hair. It's Deep Hair. It's mean hair, desperate hair, protective hair. Masculine hair. It makes my otherwise denuded pubis suddenly remind me of an old lover's beard after three or four days. And not a *good* old lover. It's the ghost of the generic shitty old lover, the one who dumped me or ignored me or forgot to call me back for days that turned into months that turned into forever.

The tuft is dug in like a Jungian animus, an archetypical Shadow, like something that only shows its face in a dark and secret place. The tuft annoys and distracts and infuriates me. It winds its roots around the base of my spinal cord and threatens to take out my entire skeleton if I dare remove it.

I'm avoiding her question. I'm thinking that maybe she wants to know if I'm actually a porn star and the need is a professional one. That's kind of flattering, if unrealistic. Or maybe she wants to know why I want the tuft off when everyone else in the world keeps and tends to their tuft. Maybe I'm a freak to hate my tuft. Maybe everyone else's tuft is lovely and soft and feminine and I'm the only one with a wild boar between my legs.

I finally answer the question by telling her the story of the lover who started the whole shaving thing. He denuded me one night and then dumped me the next day. Antonia The Skin Goddess is properly horrified. Yes, I say, not only did he shave me and dump me, he proceeded to take up immediately with another person we work with and flaunted it in front of me for the next few weeks.

Oh. Antonia The Skin Goddess is definitely on my side for this one. And, it's true, I realize, glowing in her indignation. For two weeks after, I had to watch him carry on with another girl who was visiting from out of town. He never saw fit to tell her he was involved with me. He was silent; they went out; I itched madly. I cried and went down to my car and beat up my steering wheel and kicked the walls inside the stairwells and by the time I was able to talk to him again, it was over and I hated his guts in a way that I'd never hated anyone's guts before in my life.

The whole time I was discovering my Inner Bitch Goddess and trying to crawl into my headphones at work and turning up the Rolling Stones to a volume certainly not approved by the AMA, my little pubic hair was madly trying to regain its former lush luster. Oh yeah. It was growing with a vengeance. It felt like poison oak, then straight pins, then razor blades. When I thought no one was looking, I started humping the edges of tables and the corners of walls. Then I didn't care if anyone was looking. The second I'd hit the bathroom, I pulled down the zipper on my jeans and scratch like an old grandpa kickin' back in front of the general store, and keep scratching until I'd open the door to go back out.

I decided that all my problems would be solved if I could only get Clean and Smooth.

So I went on the Internet. Looked at the dozens of

products designed to remove hair. You can buy gold-plated epilators that spin around and yank each hair out as you move across it. (User reviews included phrases like "took me two hours to do two inches" and "nearly passed out" and "if you can get past the pain it works great.")

You can buy creams and gels with names like *Cootchie Cream* and *Bare Booty Wax*. There are hot waxes and cold salves and shavers and razors contoured "with a woman's shape in mind." You can spend $80 on a multi-layered ergonomic shaver or you can go get a "Brazilian wax" for $55 (which made me think that for *sure* you'd come out looking like the Girl from Ipanema complete with admiring men, a bitchin' tan, a 1960's soundtrack and a sweet little sarong.)

My brain reeled. For days I perused web sites obsessively, and then quizzed my girlfriends at work about their technique—down to frequency, stroke pattern, and how to deal with Unfortunate Side Effects (like redness and itching and the nasty little red bumps that made the entire region about as sexy as a somewhat warty tangerine rind.)

This was all new to me, but suddenly I realized it was probably common knowledge to Every Woman Out There. It was like all the grownup women in the world knew the mysteries of exfoliation and epilation and depilatories and moisturizing just as intimately as all the grownup men in the world knew the perfect way to make Cary Grant-era concoctions named Manhattans and Highballs. I was a six year old again, standing at the edge of my parent's party while everyone spoke in an off-handed way on things about which I knew absolutely *nothing.*

Hair was growing on people and annoying them in places I'd never thought about. Back hair, chest hair, ear hair, facial hair. And as fast as the stuff was curling up out of the epidermis, people were working on removing it. All sorts of people want to remove their hair for all sorts of reasons. Athletes wanted it gone to eliminate wind resistance; old men wanted it gone to simulate youth. Women wanted it gone so they'd be smooth to the touch like a pair of silk stockings. I wanted it gone … why? Just to have it *gone.*

I purchased a set of creams designed to remove the stuff permanently, and had the smarts (after it arrived) to refrain from opening the bottles, figuring that maybe, someday, I may want the hair back. I bought a shaver. I spent long stretches in the bathroom with a pair of tweezers from my Swiss Army knife, pulling out each tenacious wire with agonizing slowness, working until my body cramped, only to look up and realize that after fifteen minutes I'd cleared an area approximately a quarter inch in diameter. Suddenly my pubic region assumed vast proportions; I felt like a pioneer looking out over my quarter section of homestead, realizing the whole thing had to be cleared out with a teaspoon.

Then, one kid-free Friday night, I hit the local Rite Aid. I'd been obsessing about the issue all week and finally decided that before I buy the "works great if you can stand the pain" $80 epilator, I'd see what the shelves held. Feeling very practical and proud of my new incremental approach to the problem, I stood in front of a section of depilatories and gels. There were about a dozen versions of Nair, which reminded me of high school commercials and Annette Funicello showing off her sleek legs in the latest 60's bathing suit.

Nair for the Hair. Sounded like a fine, practical idea. And here was a formula especially made for the "bikini area." With my new arsenal of euphemisms, I now knew what "bikini area" really stood for. Yup. I was entering the world of Every Woman Out There and learning the lingo fast.

So I picked that up. Then I saw some tubes of stuff geared to alleviate the bumps, redness and "discomfort from shaving." See? I chided myself. These are not new issues. You are not the only one. So many people have dealt with this in the world that they are making products designed with just these problems in mind. So I picked up a gel that would prevent infection, cool the area, and immediately stop the pain due to "hair removal." Neato.

Excited, I drove home. It was a Friday night, I had time to muck around in the world of feminine self-care, and I was going to emerge in a short time with a Clean Smooth twat and I could stop the madness once and for all.

I went upstairs, lined up my products, and stripped down. And, being a good documentation expert, I read all the directions. I wasn't going to be like all those other girly-girls in the world, just slapping it on any old way.

Nope, I was going to approach this in an intellectual, methodical, sensible fashion.

Well, mostly. I didn't have time to do the patch test they advocated. That's for those silly women who have sensitive skin and haven't driven a truck all over the freaking Midwest (i.e., it was for wimps). I knew I was cool enough not to have sensitive skin. And when I finally did slather the stuff on, I realized that my Wild Boar hair was going to need a few extra minutes of depilation, just to really get into the roots. So I left it on, well, perhaps a tad too long.

Sure, it stung. It was supposed to sting. Meant it was working. And yeah, my skin turned a fiery red almost immediately: another good sign. But the problem first started to manifest when I tested a little corner to see if the hair was just going to slide right out—and saw most of my skin coming off on my finger. Not the hair, mind you: just the skin.

It took me a few extra minutes to realize that it was still digging its way into the core of my body while I was gently trying to rinse it off. I tried a washcloth but it pulled off more skin. So I started, with increasing haste, to start rinsing it off, splashing water all over the floor.

Did it hurt? Ah. Yeah.

About fifteen minutes later, there I stood, with a pubis that looked for all the world like the back of those baboons in the zoo. Bright red, shiny with peeled skin, and yes, quite a bit of hair still happily manifesting itself throughout the region.

I sizzled. I oozed. I stared at myself in the mirror and

thought, man, I've done it this time.

But, help was at hand—right? I had the miracle tube of stuff that "instantly alleviated the pain of hair removal." So I squeezed the stuff generously onto my fingers and slathered that on top of the disaster.

That is when I nearly hit the roof. *That* stuff is what they use on fajitas to keep them burning as the waiter carries them all the way to the table. *That* stuff is what they used to exfoliate Vietnam. It dug into the newly flayed layers of skin and started tunneling down, looking for bone marrow. And it never actually quit doing its work: it burrowed into the smoking ruins and searched out the last remnants of living cell tissue, glorying in whatever further destruction it could mete out.

I rinsed it off, but it was too late. I could not sit. I could not walk. I could certainly not ever wear clothing again. Ohhhhhhhhh yeah. I'd done it this time.

As soon as I could talk, walk and function again (thank God it was a weekend without the kids), I realized I would probably survive. My hair survived, too. And kept growing. But after that incident I went a little bit easier on the obsession. I shaved and got frustrated and (several times) ended up with the electric shaver at 4:30 in the morning, having just found One Little Spot that needed cleaning up. But I was OK. I realized the ability to walk and wear clothing was a pretty good thing to have as one moves through the world.

Suddenly the $55 Brazilian wax jobs seemed like a bargain. And if you look around, you can find them for less. Finally I heard about Antonia The Skin Goddess. I let the stuff grow to the requisite quarter-inch and then went for a visit.

Daub daub daub, peel peel peel. A quick conversation. Feminine empathy. And we were done. Smooth and clean and lovely. I could have the tuft, or not. I could make the tuft look like a heart for Valentine's day if I wanted. I was in control!

I was impressed. So *this* is what all those Other Women know about. You just go and pay an expert to take it off.

One day I heard that the guy who started all this, the shave and run guy, was going overseas to see his latest girlfriend. I realized I had something that could come in handy for them both. I went into his office and gave him a brown paper bag, waiting a moment so I could watch him open it up.

He pulled it out and looked at me quizzically. It was the nearly-full bottle of Nair and the after-shave Agent Orange.

I told him they work best if left on a little longer than directed.

Aphrodite high-fived me on the way out.

Citizens of Different Countries

I had lunch with Evan today. About a year to the day since he met Jessica and dumped me. In the last year he has managed to lose his job, total his car and break his hand when he punched a wall in frustration. In the last year he *may* have learned that life cannot be planned with any high degree of certainty. In the last year he *may* have grown up a little bit.

Evan is 20 years younger than I am. Actually, 20 years, three months and fourteen days. And every time I see him I'm struck again by how totally *not* insane our relationship was. It made a lot of sense, why we adored each other so completely.

There are all sorts of assumptions made about relationships with such a huge age difference: We'd like different kinds of music. We'd be comfortable in completely different settings. He'd be so unschooled in the refinements of the world that I couldn't take him anywhere. He'd be scorned for being seen in public with someone who looks like his mother.

Every one of these assumptions proved untrue. We were attracted to each other *because* of our tastes in music, not despite of. Everything from Eminem to Verdi, from the Fight Club sound track to Charlie Parker. I introduced him to Garbage; he introduced me to Dre. We saw *La Bohème* together at the Met, and were both moved to tears. Nobody laughed at the way we looked together because we looked *good.*

We dressed up. We dressed down. We took long drives up PCH to eat fish tacos and drink beer. I did not radiate in his youthful light; nor did he deepen and grow beneath my wise benevolence. Nope. We were equally hot and bothered. The sun shone mutually upon both of us.

The day I was assigned to share his office, we decided to put up love beads and a yin/yang symbol. He cranked up the volume on his working music, and I loved it. We'd been friends before; now we were office mates. It was an auspicious start.

He was model-quality handsome, with huge dark eyes, curly brown hair and a constant three-day growth of beard. I'd listen to his tales every morning: the girls, the drinking, more girls. He played saxophone. He was a black belt in aikido and we practiced throws and grappling locks on each other between meetings. I knew he was trouble the first time I sat in his car and he cranked up his $6000 sound system and I felt my fillings start to rattle. I'm a total sucker for a big woofer, and big woofers are what Evan is all about.

In our rambling conversations he taught me the finer points of lying, and we'd discuss the moral implications of the various crazy situations he'd get himself into. We'd laugh at all the women he was deceiving; then we'd get serious and talk about his dreams. And I'd sit on the other side of the office, smiling to myself, thinking how very different his reality was from mine with the kids, the school, the bills, the responsibilities.

Once we started the conversation by email, the whole thing changed. Words, of course, are my favorite sandbox to play in, and I'm a sucker for anyone who knows the same games I do. He got my nuances almost immediately and knew when to play and when to take me seriously. He was *quick*. And he was smart. I introduced him to the Castaneda 'path with heart' essay and he got it. We discussed theories of consciousness and he'd tell me of experiments and articles that supplemented the things I'd been reading about. We didn't have to fill in any blanks, even at the start. We began with shorthand, and then went deeper.

He didn't mind going to the deep waters with me. In fact, he insisted upon it. Pretty soon we were talking on the phone on the way to work and emailing or instant messaging each other at work. We went out to lunch and continued the conversation. After work, we'd keep going. If we weren't talking a mile a minute about something we both felt was vitally important, we felt like we were wasting valuable time. And when it got sexual, our intercourse simply turned non-verbal, and the communication continued.

"What would you *talk* about?" I hear people say, when presented with the idea of going out with someone even ten years younger. That was never our problem. He told me he felt he had finally found someone who understood his language. And I felt the same way. I don't think it was an age thing at all; it was who he was and who I was. It just worked.

So what was the problem? Well, we *were* 20 years apart in age. And that difference manifested itself in ways I could never have predicted. It was not that we were strangers. It was more that we were from different cultures. And the biggest difference was that I had been to his country, but he had never been to mine.

Little things brought out the difference. Like the $6000 sound system. In *his* country he still had a concept called "expendable income." He lived in the house he grew up in, with his mother. That was like finding out my lover regularly ate monkey brains for afternoon tea.

And he thought that life could be planned. We would talk for hours about how his career would go and how he would be making *x* amount of money in *y* amount of years. I would frown, inwardly, thinking about what a cynical loser I had become, wondering when I had lost my own ability to dream and plan and count on life in such an assured fashion.

Then I'd mention this part of his personality to my girlfriends and they would crumple over, laughing their asses off. Gasping for breath, they'd sputter the words "life ... " and then gasp " ... *planned*?!!!" And then, finally, I'd laugh along until the tears squeezed out of our eyes and we'd wave our hands lamely at each other, begging the other to look the other way so we could catch our breath.

Life could be planned: only someone from his country could entertain a notion that sweetly far-fetched.

When things fell apart, they did so quickly and without warning. He had been seeing one of his old girlfriends throughout our affair and had, of course, lied with a master's precision about it. He picked up the new one, Jessica, while he and I were in Boston for the holidays and I had gone off for a couple of hours to do something with my kids. About a month later, he decided she should move out here to California so they could live together.

I was enraged. Not only was I now suddenly without

a really great companion, I was now officially one of the girls he giggled about lying to.

It helped that their relationship was a spectacular disaster. It helped that he totaled his car. It helped that he'd call me for advice when things went south, which they did on a regular basis. It all helped. But it didn't change the cold hard fact that he simply had some growing up to do. And it wasn't going to be on my shift.

Perhaps it's just the universe punishing him for breaking my heart (at least, I hope it is), but today at lunch I didn't hear him talking that convincingly about his latest life plan. His new car (now seven months old) is still sporting dealer stickers instead of plates. I suspect that Evan has crossed a barrier between knowing what life is all about to being just a bit hesitant about putting his weight fully down.

I love the view from where I am. I have two children who expand my horizons every single day. I have felt the monsoon rains on my face and heard the flutes of Bangkok floating in the twilight. I will always have had two decades' more life and love and heartache and joy than he ever will.

We could talk about his dreams, and I could tell him what things looked like from the top of my mountain, but no matter what journey we could possibly take together, my perspective will always be irrevocably different. I have been to his country and what I don't know about it I can understand. But he will never know what it is like to be in mine, and by the time he gets here, I'll be off exploring some new uncharted territory of my own.

The Delicate Art of Lying

"The secret of success is sincerity. Once you can fake that you've got it made."

Jean Giraudoux

I *asked my ex-husband Tom*—who no longer has much reason to be anything but honest with me—why men lie. He said he didn't know, but they only do it when their lips move.

There is a great art to lying and I've had the questionable privilege of associating with some world-class masters in the field.

I learned a lot about the art the night I discovered my Inner Bitch Goddess. I had been having increasingly bad interactions with a guy I was seeing at work. It culminated in a series of unanswered pages and miscommunications. After the last one, I left the office, kicked the shit out of a perfectly innocent marble wall in the parking lot, and cursed men at the top of my lungs as I drove out of the lot burning rubber around the curves.

On the way home I called Evan, my ex-turned-confidante, who wasn't picking up. I screamed a voice message to him, hung up, and promptly redialed as I thought of even more reasons to yell at him. I repeated the cycle several times until he called back.

Once I stopped accusing him of being the source of all that is wrong with the world and men and my life, we finally got down to it. Evan's a liar. Everyone acknowledges that. The guy at work, I felt, was also lying to me, although I couldn't pin him down on anything. I suddenly wondered how much Tom had lied to me. And … Gregg, my first boyfriend … had he lied? I realized that I had no clue whatsoever about anything any more. I felt like I was tangled in so many webs of deceit that I'd never feel safe with anyone ever again.

So I asked him. What is it about lying? What's this thing about? How come men are so fucking *good* at it?[1] What I got was enough information to put together a little primer on the delicate art of lying.

---

1 OK, in truth and fairness, women are pretty good at it, too. I have to admit that as we talked for the next two hours, I exhibited some flair in the art form myself. However, since this story comes out of some pretty amazing interactions with the best in the lying biz (all men), I'm going to keep it simple and continue to apply the masculine pronoun.

Why do men lie?

They have one thing on their mind

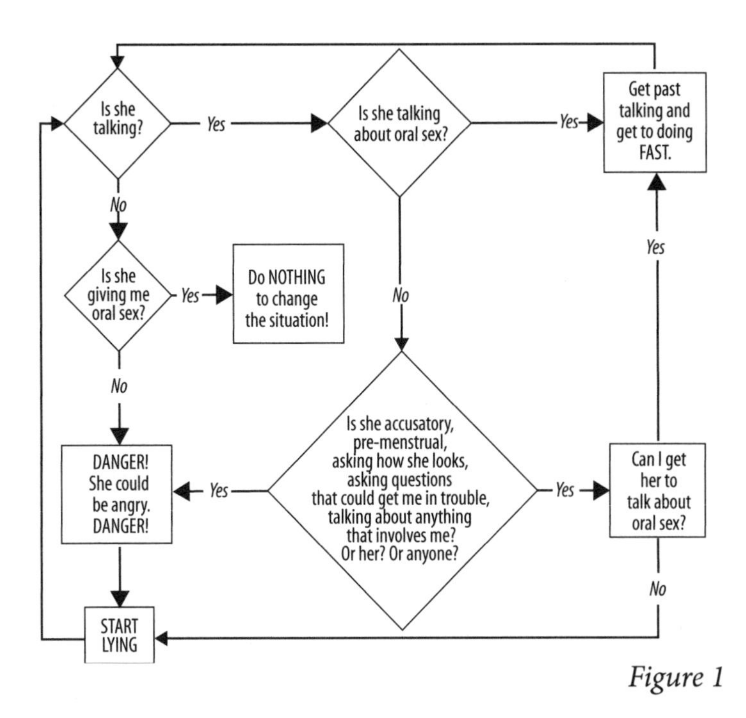

Figure 1

To understand why men lie, you have to understand the prime interest of a man: oral sex. I believe that oral sex informs pretty much of all male behavior. (Please see *Figure 1*, above.)

Men really want to avoid anything that's going to get in between them and oral sex. So pissing us off is one of the things they want to avoid the most. Hence the lying.

To avoid getting busted

In order to get the most oral sex possible, it's imperative for a man to never (or rarely) get in trouble with us. And let's be honest, oh my sisters. We are *good* at busting a man. We have a bad day at work because our boss is an anal-retentive freak? We go home and bust the boyfriend for not putting the laundry away. We find out we have to spend $700 on a timing belt for our Honda? We go home and bust the husband for not making enough money to buy us a new BMW just like the one our office-mate's husband just bought for her. We feel fat? Obviously his fault for giving us a bad body image. We have PMS, a hangnail, a bad hair day? We bust him for that, too. Just because.

I would venture to say, based on some conversations I've overheard, that we are as good at busting a guy as he is at fibbing his way out of a situation. (And we think this is a *coincidence*?)

So what do we expect? We spend half our lives busting men over nothing, so if and when they finally *do* do something they're going to lie their asses off. They've seen the consequences for *nothing* so *something* is going to be a whole lot worse.

It is a sad fact that we women are not perfect. It's OK that we're not perfect because of the oral sex factor (i.e., they wouldn't put up with us for a second if they could reach that enticing member all by themselves), but in general I believe a man would rather lie than get busted so they can stay on our good side (if and when that good side ever actually shows up).

The Fine Line

Before he starts a lie, a man needs to understand he's committing to walking a fine line. If he decides to cover up something he's done, he is now opening himself up to either getting busted on his crime or the lie itself.

His course of action goes back to his primary goal. He must decide what's going to get more in the way of that goal: getting nailed on the lie or getting nailed on the truth. For the dedicated pro, this is usually not too difficult a choice: at best he's wielded his sword of deception in a beautiful and effective way, at worst he's gone down in a blaze of obfuscating glory, remaining true to his Art (if not his woman).

For the neophyte liar, it's a more difficult dilemma that should be weighed carefully. Living a life of truth is admittedly a less glamorous proposition, but it is a whole lot safer. Not to mention that nasty integrity thing you get to accumulate after awhile.

Should a man go for the lie, there are some excellent ways to obscure the truth. In my opinion, outright falsehood is gutless and not recommended. The other extreme is the intricate smokescreen—in which the artisan clouds the air with so many unnecessary half-truths and quarter-truths that it is hard to focus on any one deception. The smokescreen technique takes years of practice and could be dangerous; losing track of reality is a common side effect that you'd need to discuss with a licensed therapist. You could end up having more to worry about than your girlfriend (if you still have one).

In between these extremes are some solid techniques

that many people of both genders have found indispensable over the years.

How to lie with integrity and style

Always tell the truth

There really is only one rule for world-class lying and that is to always tell the truth. True Jedi master prevaricators become so by understanding the fundamental nature of truth and then subtly changing it to meet their needs.

Telling the truth is the only way to do it right. You own the lie, you have lived the lie, you would pass a polygraph test in a heartbeat. When you tell the truth, you get the element of unshakable internal belief in your own honesty. You are convincing and you are bulletproof in your self-righteousness. The trick is in what truths to tell, and how to tell them. …

Nocturnal omissions

There are many facets to the great art of lying and most of them involved omitting some part of the truth. The classic example is the "Where were you tonight, dear?" lie.

The conversation goes like this:

"Why are you home so late, darling?"

"I'm so sorry. I had dinner with Larry [the boss] then swung by the bookstore on the way home. Check out this wireless system they're rolling out next fall …" Then the husband proceeds to pull out this week's techno-geeko-electronic gadget mag, and show his wife the latest gizmo.

Instantly bleary with boredom, she drops the issue.

All of it is true. The guy went out for dinner with his single co-workers and they bet him an apple martini that he couldn't get the cute legal assistant at that table over there to leave with him. He takes up the bet, drives her home and they have a little fun in the front seat. He swings by the local Borders bookstore to use the restroom to wash the lipstick off his belt buckle and then spends a few moments catching up, happily, with the latest electronics magazines on the shelf. His heart rate down to normal, he then drives home.

Everything he tells to his wife is true: he is sorry (that he had to come home), he did have dinner (liquid), he did stop by the bookstore (to tidy up) and then he came right home. All his actions were verifiable and true. Hearing this in his voice, and having tangible evidence in her hand, the wife probes no further and the topic is closed.

In this example, the guy is obviously a pro and has embellished the traditional response with a few special added touches. Note the non-incriminating evidence: it proves that one part of the story is true, it gives him a physical prop to produce if she starts questioning him too closely, and he's already trained her to doze off when he goes into electronics mode, so she's more than willing to escape the conversation herself.

The Optical illusion lie

Figure 2

This is a beautiful piece of work. In this lie, you create so many blocks of black that the person being deceived is convinced they see the dark gray circles in between (please see *Figure 2,* above).

Suppose a man is on a business trip in Amsterdam and needs to obscure the fact that he and his client have stopped by the red light district to smoke a little hooch. He can create an illusion of work and culture-seeking by sending emails from the office, video messages from the Van Gogh Museum and by calling his wife from the opera at night. He will talk about the work, the meetings, the tedious dinners, the beauty of the paintings and drops a hint about something he picked up for her while there.

The plethora of detail and the tangible evidence of a cultural experience should be enough to obscure the fact that he and his client knocked off work early to go hit a few pubs and then, completely stoned, swung by the gift shop at the museum for five minutes to get their respective mates a couple of refrigerator magnets. In his version, there is no room for fooling around, and he paints the beautiful, expressionistic picture that he wants.

The Confessional lie

The confessional lie should be used only when absolutely needed. It presupposes that you've done something so heinous that you're pretty sure you're going to lose the whole relationship and never get oral sex again (from this woman at least), so you brace yourself for the collateral damage and go for a huge fight and weeks of recriminations instead.

When he was two, my son Chris had a phrase he coined to describe something that was worth getting in trouble over: "maddable." If it wasn't a big deal, he'd yell in self-defense—"Mom! That wasn't maddable!"—and he was usually right. With the confessional lie, if you've done something truly maddable, what you need to do is cop to something only somewhat maddable.

Say your girlfriend has some incontrovertible evidence: a picture of you and another girl, sloppy drunk and grinning, in front of a club in Tribeca. The cousin you were with that night has a vindictive ex and she emailed it to your girlfriend. So, yeah. You're busted.

Here's what you do: Get some flowers. And be prepared to eat crow. Then cop to "everything": confess to meeting this girl while visiting your cousin three years ago in New York. You were drunk. He had dared you to hit on her. When pressed, confess that you *think* you kissed her. You can't remember anything except that you didn't enjoy it. She was fat.

Then stick to the story like glue. It's true, after all—you did kiss her (before, during and after staying up all night doing it like mad dogs in every room of her SoHo loft, including the fire escape). You didn't enjoy it (well, not as much as if her twin had actually showed up like she'd promised). And there really were, maybe, a few more ounces of fat (squeezed into her D-cups) than really should've been there. So it's all true. Just make sure to stay riveted to the story and hope your face (and other parts of your anatomy) don't betray you.

Change in time/space/events

You get the idea. A good liar can shift time and events around to suit his purposes. It's all about creating a lovely onstage magic behind which you can sneak some non-essential facts out the stage door and into the alley. There are some bits of truth that aren't strictly necessary for everyone to know, and it's better for all concerned if they don't get the bright lights shining directly in their eyes.

Last Ditch

Even Jedi masters need to learn from their mistakes, so

you will be asked direct questions from time to time. There are ways to get out of these situations gracefully, too. Here are some tricks for how to weasel out of a good honest bust without resorting to the ultimate cop-out of an outright falsity.

Act hurt

This is pretty standard and almost always works. Good phrases to use might be:

- I can't believe you'd think I'd do such a thing!
- You're killing me with these accusations!
- After all these years, I can't believe you don't trust me.
- I'm crushed.

If all else fails you can also simply stare incredulously and stalk out of the room to nurse your wounded pride.

Answer a question with a question

- What do you mean, where have I been?
- Don't you trust me?

Deflect, deflect, deflect

- What? Yeah, I went to the company party after work. The food was terrible. I missed your great cooking. Do you have any leftovers? What did you do today?

Reversal/Guilt parry

- I called you and you weren't around. Where were you?
- I'm glad you brought this up because I've been wondering a few things myself.

How to catch a liar

Before you decide to catch someone in a lie, you really need to know if he's worth the effort. Obviously, if you find yourself in anything resembling any of the situations above, you need to evaluate what you're doing with the guy in the first place. If you think you're with a true Jedi master prevaricator, I'd say dump his lying ass and hold out for a better deal.

However, if you're working on a fib (rather than a whopper) scale, and it's occasional rather than chronic, then maybe you do want to give him another chance. Or maybe it's just not that serious a relationship and you find the hunt just about as fun as he finds the chase.

There are very few situations that a great liar can't weasel his way out of. If you really want to catch someone in a falsehood, the best way to do it is to ask direct questions and keep at it. They can always resort to pure, outright dishonesty. And if you believe an outright lie, or can't tell the difference from the rest of the b.s., then you're just as far away from the truth as when you began.

So you need to keep at it to catch someone in a lie.

But this begs yet another question:

Why?

Think about it: Do you really want to hear everything that goes on in your husband's mind? Would you really want your boyfriend listening in to everything you think about all day long?

I don't think so.

I don't want to know when he's looking at my visible panty line and thinking my ass looks fatter than it did on the first date (when he thought it was a little chunky in the first place). I don't want him to know I was checking out that guy in the next booth over while he was out buying me that red rose for our third month anniversary. There are thoughts that go through our minds that other people simply don't need to know.

It takes a great amount of work to either hide or find the truth. With someone who is always on the defensive, or has been well-trained in the past, you may never get the whole story. Unless you want to buy a polygraph and really get down to the bottom of things, you're going to have to make some tough decisions.

As a daily practice, I think it's important to adopt a philosophy of assuming either guilt or innocence, and then act accordingly. If you assume guilt you can look at everything your partner says in light of this chapter and drive yourself absolutely insane. Perhaps you'll be right on occasion, but you're also going to live with a cloud of jealousy, fear and suspicion over your head.

If you assume innocence, you'll probably have a happier life. You'll probably be closer to actual trust in your relationship, and you'll probably be able to command more loyalty and honesty overall.

Before you decide whether or not to go into the lie-busting business ask yourself: Are you getting your needs met? Do you still have a connection with your partner?

If both of these were answered in the affirmative, shut up and love him openly. Assume innocence and move on. If these are not affirmative answers, you have other issues going on and it's time to start dealing with them.

Bottom Line

I had an epiphany in my 30's. I realized I was completely stressed out when driving on the freeway from always looking for cops in my rear view mirror. It struck me that if I simply drove closer to the speed limit, I could eliminate a huge source of concern from my life.

The higher road in all relationships is for both people to simply lead a more honest life. It's kind of that simple.

First, you need to keep an eye on your own speedometer. Lead your own life based on your own internal standards of honesty.

Secondly, let the speeders and prevaricators pass you by. Their decision to live dishonestly is their karma, not yours.

Third, if you're surrounded by webs of deceit, slice through them with your own clear light saber of honesty.

Finally, choose to leave the liars to their own fates and find someone who is spending more time basking in your light and less energy covering his tracks.

It boils down to trust. Not trust in the other person's perfection, but trust that the universe will tell us things on a need-to-know basis ... not before, not after, not more, not less. We have to trust that occasionally we may be told the truth. When he says he loves us. When he says he can't live without us. When he says he cares.

Live life on the trusting side. Take a moment to try to track down the truths as well.

When does a man tell the truth? It may not be every time his lips move, but it may be something you can read in his eyes, his hands and in his heart. Listen to that information carefully, for it may be telling you the actual truth. Not about what he does with his body, but what he's doing with his soul. That is equally, if not more, important.

Card-carrying Projectionist

I *am a card-carrying projectionist.* Back when there really were such things as projectionists who did change-overs and wielded carbon arcs with power and skill, I became the third woman projectionist in Northern California, member of Local 611 of the International Alliance of Theatrical Stage Employees.

Which I find very funny, as one of my favorite parts of relationships is the projection thing. I see a male of the species and, whammo, he's my dad, or my ex-husband, or some other archetype. My internal projector gets going and I use this poor unsuspecting person as my little screen.

Meanwhile he says, Hey, here's a female. Whee! I'll bet she's *just* like my mom *and* my sister *and* that little hottie I remember from seventh grade. So he goes to town with *his* projector. And we flash shadows on each other like mad fools, drop them when it comes time for some animalistic rutting in the sack, and then pick them back up again as soon as the sweat dries off.

The first acts of these movies are always exquisite. Our thoughts merge seamlessly, the sex is better than any sex ever experienced by anyone in the history of the world, we are so *totally* each other's other halves that it's scary.

And then there's That Moment. Where I'm suddenly and inexplicably confounded by who I'm looking at. We've been going out a month, two months, maybe even six … and then one day I look at this person and suddenly *see* him.

And he's not all that great. In fact, he's barely even recognizable. Here I am glorying in the lovely transparency between our souls—and suddenly I realize he's Someone Else. He doesn't finish my sentences as though he's reading my mind after all; that trait of his is actually called "interrupting." He does things that I'd *never* do, or (worse) he does things *exactly* like I do. Or maybe I never knew it, but he's a … Republican! It's awful. It's messy and awkward and my heart sinks. He is just another person. Like me.

What I want is that first reel back. The cool one where the sex is always great and we can talk all night (about *nothing*!) and come out feeling whole and fabulous and loved down to our electrons. But ya know what? That movie is over. Won't come back. Well, not for a long while.

So I sit there across from him realizing I've never set eyes on him before in my life. What the hell do I do?

If I stop the projector, turn on the lights and take a long hard look at the situation, I am confronted with the daunting and unromantic task of getting to know another, separate human being. This is a person who is *not* me and never will be. This person can and will bore me senseless. This person will mispronounce words and have little quirks that will slowly and inexorably drive me completely insane.

This person will be sweet at times, glorious even. We may still talk for hours into the night, but when we wake up together we're going to have to face the same old world that I'd hoped I'd left behind forever when we first met. Bills will still need to be paid. The commute will still suck. Alone in our own private hells, we will still have to deal with the DMV.

I don't have any answers. I have seen couples who have succeeded in going through this phase and many others, and they have reached a true intimacy after many years. That intimacy is a lot like that first intimacy, except it's deeper, better, based on real understanding.

And it's not just about how long you manage to stick together. The people I know who have this true intimacy are different from other couples. They look into each other's eyes when they talk. They listen to the other person and genuinely laugh at their jokes. Even after many years of being together. It's super cool. And I don't think it happens unless you get extremely lucky and work extremely hard.

So there are three scenarios possible.

First, we can live out a series of fabulous and captivating first acts. They contain all the elements: the first meeting, the coming together, the setup for a great adventure to come. But when something happens to cause a bit of reality to leak into the picture, the film breaks and we change to another storyline.

Or we get stuck in a long second act. Reality is all too apparent but the plot is never furthered. The excitement of the setup is long forgotten. And the final credits are boringly remote. This second act scenario seems to be where most marriages linger for years. It's certainly where mine was before the stranger rode into town and changed the plot line for good.

With luck though, we sometimes make it to a great third act that doesn't actually end with everyone in tears. Sometimes we find someone truly worthy with whom to go through all this. And with tenacity on both parts, it is possible, I think, to work through the obstacles of the second and create a third act that actually contains within it the seeds for a glorious sequel. A sequel that is so good that it goes on to inspire the next sequel, and the next—all different, all deeper, all glorious. Same cast; different layers, different arcs, different meanings.

That's what I'm looking for. A fully intertwined story. A mutual projection that will go on and on, always changing, always interesting and never fully resolving into boredom and complacency. I need someone who won't collapse the first time he sees me for who I really am. I want someone with whom—even when I see his own flaws and inconsistencies—I can still spin out reels of great movies, reveling in the same joy as when the curtain first opened.

Living Life Deliberately

I went to the woods because I wished to live deliberately, to front only the essential facts of life, and see if I could not learn what it had to teach, and not, when I came to die, discover that I had not lived.

Henry David Thoreau

S*everal years ago I executed* a glorious experiment in the name of living life deliberately: I withdrew a sizeable chunk out of my retirement savings, decided to take my unemployment as a call to adventure, stopped looking for work, and spent two months following a few simple rules:

- I would act as if money were not a limiting factor.
- I wouldn't do anything with my time that I wasn't willing to do for the rest of my life.

- I would limit my time doing "daily life tasks" to only a few hours a day.

Rather than spending most of my time doing laundry, paying bills, going to a job I hated (or looking for a new job to hate), and then doing what mattered most in the time left over (which was nil), I flipped the ratio. I did what mattered first, and kept the daily minutiae confined to a certain limited period of time.

Now, of course, the not-going-to-the-job part couldn't last forever. Although it was a limited experiment, I learned a lot in those two months. I now believe it's possible to live life deliberately on an everyday basis, with children, with a job, with responsibilities. It doesn't necessarily require independent wealth or an indefinite vacation.

It's not easy, given the culture we live in and the churn surrounding us. But it's possible and the ways to explore the concept are limitless. Even when crazed. Even when busy. Even now.

I returned from Christmas vacation this year utterly spent. I was exhausted and daunted as I looked towards the next year of work, kids, trying to exercise, trying to maintain a few friendships, trying to stay sane. I realized that my head was bursting at the seams with endless "shoulds" and "shouldn'ts." So I sat down and wrote all of it down, just to see what my inner voice mail was recording every minute of the day.

I filled up three pages without even coming up for air. I should lose weight. I should do a better job at work. I should work harder with the kids on cub scout activities. I should write thank you notes going back at least six months. I should spend more time alone. I should spend more time with friends. I should be more disciplined in my life. I should relax. I should get up early and write. I should stay up late and write. I should get more sleep. I should quit saying I should all the time.

Wow. No wonder I'm wiped out. My brain is continually teeming with this *list*. Where does it all come from?

I looked at the list more carefully and realized most of these thoughts come from fear. Fear of missing some important part of the kids' lives. Fear of what other people will think of me. Fear of financial difficulty. Fear of letting things get out of control. Fear of failure.

Even that revelation wasn't the worst of it. I realized that anything I started to do to fix it ended up containing that dreaded word again: I should not worry so much, I should accept that this is the way it is, I should just Let It Go.

What a mess.

There has to be some way around this, I thought. I

looked at the list again. What if I replaced the shoulds with the word want? What would that do to the list?

Well, that was harder than it looked. When I got right down to it, I wanted all of it. I wanted sleep *and* exercise *and* to be a better mother *and* lots more time to do nothing. So, in the big picture, that didn't work at all.

But what about the smaller picture? What about just doing what I wanted to do *right now*? Would the world collapse? Would I end up sleeping all day, watching soap operas and eating bon bons? Would I become some horrible future feature on the *Jerry Springer Show* ("She Lived Life Deliberately And See What Happened")? Well, except for the fact that I hate soap operas, it seemed like a very real possibility.

But come on. Really? Would I really just disintegrate if I started doing the "I wants" before the "I shoulds"? I don't know. But it's an interesting thought. Very interesting.

Joseph Campbell, who seems to know what he's talking about, talks about following your bliss. And I know there are amazing people who have done that and changed the world in significant ways. So maybe it's not about doing what I should, or not about doing what I shouldn't, but maybe it could be about doing what I *love*.

Maybe doing what I love is a better algorithm for figuring out how to spend my time, rather than following a checklist of items that come from ancient anxieties. Every one of the shoulds seemed to come from a place of fear rather than desire or bliss.

So that's my goal for today. To operate from a position of what I want to *be*, rather than operating from an endless list of what I need to *do*. To look at every situation and assess whether I'm doing this out of fear or desire. Take it moment by moment and see if it works any better than letting the list of shoulds rule me.

That's my goal. And I'll start just as soon as I finish the dishes. I really should try to get the kids to school on time.

Mommy Pow

My son Jack first brought up the idea because Vin Diesel looks sooo awesome on his snowboard in *XXX*. Then Chris chimed in. Then another hip young friend of mine, Sam, mentioned it. That year we had decent snow, and there was a resort nearby with relatively affordable rates and a great kid's academy. I said "OK, let's do it." So we planned a day on the slopes.

Before you discover this for yourself, let me tell you right off that I am pretty uncool. For one thing, I'm a mom, which is considered in many circles to be the definition of uncool. Secondly, on my first day on the slopes in, ahem, about 25 years, I opted to ski instead of snowboard. According to my sons and Sam, skiing is very uncool when compared to snowboarding. (Either is cooler than being a mom.)

Thirdly—and this is the part I didn't completely cop to publicly when we were planning this excursion—I was never any good, even back in the dawn of time when I last nervously climbed into a chairlift and tumbled down the three-degree slope when dismounting. In my opinion, being untalented and uncoordinated is about as uncool as it gets.

The biggest issue was whether I was going to ski or snowboard. The kids wanted me to learn to snowboard with them and I figured I didn't have much relearning to do since I'd never known what I was doing on skis anyway. Sam, being young and a snob, was also insistent that I try snowboarding. However, two of my other close friends—about my age and in pretty good shape—told me that snowboarding was the hardest thing they'd ever done and that they'd hated it.

I finally decided I'd go for the known quantity of skiing. And thus I endured a good morning's worth of ridicule and taunting from all three of my cold-hearted companions.

When we arrived the problems really started. An expensively clad woman took about 15 minutes at the ticket window in front of us, haggling about her discount coupons. Renting the snowboard stuff took forever. Then Sam decided to bond with the kids by making fun of me for forcing everyone to stand in the ski line after they were done.

Then, when I got my uncool stuff, my uncool ski boots hurt. My uncool skis were heavy. The uncool poles were cumbersome. After we had hiked up to the top of a small hill, we realized that Jack had dropped his glove at the bottom of the hill and I had to trudge back down to get it. Sam mentioned that I really needed to get my sense of humor back.

By this time I remembered all too well why I never was very good at skiing: I hated it. I really did. It was clumsy and stupid and I like friction. I did not like wrapping my feet up in tight boots and strapping long slippery sticks on them and pointing downhill. I don't care how cool it looks from the outside, I just didn't like it.

But I was there so I figured I only had to endure the next five hours or so. So I packed the kids into the ski school and prepared to start confronting my own demons.

What a relief when I realized that in the past quarter century someone had actually figured out how to make putting skis on easier. I remember hopping along after my skis as one or the other slid downhill, hoping that when it impaled someone it would do a good enough job to kill them outright rather than leave them a worthless (and litigious) vegetable. Now there are the nifty little brakes that dig into the snow while you get your boot in the binding. That was a good start.

After we geared up, Sam and I headed off to the chairlift for the easiest slopes. I eyed it nervously. I remembered from bitter experience how daunting it could be to be up there on a "bunny" slope and have no clue how to get back to the nice warm lodge except by inching down on my butt. Humiliating and uncomfortable and cold.

I scanned the deepest recesses of my imagination for a decent excuse as we stood in the line to the chairlift. I began to get really annoyed at every human being in sight. I also started freaking out. As I said earlier, I was never very good in the dismount department. With eyes sharpened by fear, I stared up at the far end of the lift, watching people ski or snowboard off of it. I scanned all the instructions for getting on and off the lift, and wondered if my fear of heights had become better or worse over the years.

I talked to myself rationally, saying that the worst that could happen is that I'll look like a total jerk in front of my cute young friend (who really wasn't that great a friend anyway, come to think of it, because what kind of friend would drag me into something like this?) Maybe the lift will have to stop while I disentangle myself. And maybe I'll break a few bones. That's the worst that could happen. Death was probably not a likely possibility. So I gamely slid through the gate, repositioned my uncool poles to my inside hand, grabbed the outside strut of the lift, and got on.

Ahhhh. I'm on the lift and I'm suddenly in old psychological territory: that moment I know, without a doubt, that I cannot stop fate from doing what it will to me. I am stuck in a precarious situation and have no control over the matter. I both hate and love that psychic landscape. I seek it out as eagerly as I fear it. It tells me I'm on the edge, I'm pushing my own internal limits, that something *new* is going to happen and, no matter how stupid I was to get into this situation to begin with, it's too late to stop now.

The end of the lift is in sight. A sign says to raise the tips of my skis and prepare to dismount. I lift my tips. I prepare. I take a deep breath … and sail down the incline, balancing my weight squarely over my insteps, gliding onto the snow and coming to a nice stop.

Wow.

Where did I learn to do *that*? I wonder. That was …that was *good*. I take a deep breath, square my shoulders and face the next step. Going *down* the hill.

First there's this issue of all the cool snowboarders. Man, they're all over the place, hopping around after getting off the lift, dragging their boards with one foot and humping to the top of the slope. Then they stand around hunched over fiddling with their bindings to get their other foot latched in.

Maybe I'm not getting something, but there's something about lugging 12 pounds of fiberglass and then hopping around on one foot that seems, well, kind of clumsy. Like, not that graceful. Or, let's face it … *cool*.

I navigate around all the Quasimodo's and position myself at the top of the slope. I intellectually remember the physics of digging into the snow with the edge of my skis and bear in mind that even though it looks dorky, I can always snowplow all the way down. I can even resort to sitting on my butt and inching if it comes to that.

But, speaking of butts … there seemed to be a lot of butt-sitting on the slope directly below me. The cool snowboarders seemed to spend a lot of time sitting on their butts in the middle of the slope. I don't know whether this is proper etiquette or not, and I'm sure it's definitely a function of being on a beginner's slope—but on that run on that day they were scattered around like they were having picnics. Clusters of snow-squatters just sitting around chatting. I thought, huh, this is interesting. Back in the stone ages, when we were all uncool skiers, we actually could go *down* the slope without doing a slalom course around a bunch of inanimate bodies. But … whatever. I'm obviously not getting it yet.

I start down and to my intense surprise I am able to navigate pretty well. I ski around the snowboarders sitting around on their butts. I traverse and ski back around the snowboarders who are flinging themselves over on their stomachs like turtles and trying to push their way up. I come back again and pass my hip young friend pushing his way up, only to fall down again 20 seconds later. Meanwhile I swish around back and forth around them and suddenly … it's OK.

I'm OK.

This is … this is kind of fun.

From then on, the day was a joy. I became sure of myself. We attempted more difficult runs. I kept up with Sam. I waved to my kids down at the ski school. I took a class myself and was put in the advanced group.

I was awesome. I rocked. I'd never skied better in my life. My mind was confident and relaxed, and my body could execute maneuvers that I never thought I could possibly do in this lifetime.

And all the while I was thinking what is *this* all about?

I'm old, I've had kids, and I was pathetic to begin with. Where did all this *skill* come from?

First. It ain't about age, baby. As George Harrison says in *Yellow Submarine*: it's all in the mind. It's nice to have a fit young body, but it's way more important to have a fit and agile mind. In the past three years I'd learned martial arts. My body had acquired, through arduous drill and discipline, enough muscle memory to start working well on an unconscious level. I'd learned how to roller blade. I'd taken up boogie boarding. I'm no longer (totally) afraid of pain, I know how to fall, and I actually love the feeling of pushing my body to its furthest limit.

Is this a function of a young body or an eager mind? I would suggest the latter. My body had irrefutably aged 25 years since the last time I was on skis. But my mind had embraced new concepts and taught my body how to rethink some of its old, limiting precepts. The difference was revolutionary.

Second. Fear is the only adversary on the mountain. It's not you vs. the mountain or the ice patches or the degree of incline. It's you vs. your innermost demon: fear.

I was riding up the lift and watching the snowboarders (on a more advanced slope, the ones not on their butts still trying to look cool) rocket down the hill. Whoosh. Man, they looked *good*—full tilt, catching air, looking like they've never done anything other than move at 70 mph on slippery surfaces with their feet strapped onto a big board their whole lives. What was the difference between them and me and my conservative traverses?

Well, besides skill and experience, it was mainly *cojones*. They had dealt with and conquered their fear. They were not interested in reasserting, at every turn, their ability to *stop*. They were in control and they were enjoying the ride.

So I used that and recalibrated my thought process: rather than testing to see if I could stop, maybe I could test to see if I was under control. If I wasn't in any imminent danger of falling or running into something, it wasn't necessary to prove to myself again and again that I could stop. It was only necessary to keep safe and enjoy myself.

Fear is the mountain we're skiing on and against. The snow, the equipment, our bodies, our techniques and the mountain itself are all allies we can use to conquer the true enemy. The point, however, is not to decide to be fearless, point your feet downhill and just *go*. The point is to truly harness all the skills and to understand the allies to such maximum advantage that you truly don't have the fear any more.

All that glorious day I rode the lift up and worked mind, body and spirit on the way down. I waved to my kids below, watching them also go from butt-sitting to taking some pretty good runs.

The best moment came sitting on the lift with Chris. We were stopped and swung our skis (and board) back and forth slightly to see if we could hit the skiers down below with the snow we knocked off. We pointed at some snowboarders and commented on their form. We counted five wipeouts before we started moving again. We compared thoughts on granularity, I explained wind chill, and we gauged the length of the shadows to figure out how many runs we could get in before it started to ice up. We were two people engaged in a new activity; there was perfect harmony in the world.

When I got home I instantly logged on to the Internet and checked out the weather report: a new storm coming in, fresh Mother Nature Powder. (The kids on the forum affectionately call it Mommy Pow.) And the next day, sore and aching and utterly invigorated, I took the kids to the local Sports Chalet, whipped out the credit card, and bought us all our own equipment. Because we're doing this again. Soon.

Mommy Pow, here I come.

Grace Notes

T*o paraphrase Carl Sandburg,* grace comes by on little cat feet. Grace rarely makes for very good stories. Because grace creates sweet moments, and small.

A few years back I flew to Wichita, Kansas to do a few shows with the opera company I work with. The company was arriving the next day; as the technical director I had advanced them so I'd have time to set up the theatre.

The young man sitting next to me on the plane offered to drive me to the hotel. We ended up stopping for a beer at a sports bar with a couple of his friends, and the evening took off from there.

My seatmate was married, one of the other guys was a

studly young man with a strong jaw and a twinkle in his eye. The third man was slightly more weathered, with a barely-concealed sadness lurking in his face whenever he turned the animation off. I am an expert at spotting a mid-life crisis a mile off. At a certain point I decided to stop the chit-chat and start talking to that one for real. It was a good connection.

That night I was Dorothy escorted through Kansas accompanied by my three trusty companions. I was safe, I was adored, and they laughed at my jokes. They plied me with their local brews and danced me around more dance floors than I can remember.

The midlife crisis guy was a great dancer. Our fates were sealed, at least for one evening.

Flash forward one week. I'm back in L.A., at a girlfriend's party. My cell phone rings: it was the Wichita guy. He was unexpectedly in California and called to see what I was doing. I left to go find him down at the beach. Using our cell phones, routed through Kansas, he navigated me into the parking lot where he stood waiting for me. We ordered a beer and tried to figure out how it was we were hanging out together in a bar in Redondo Beach, California.

After a beer or two, we wandered out to the sand and sat on a bench, the warm breezes of summer ruffling our hair. Suddenly, he was down on his knees. He was not in California accidentally. He had come to see me. My heart ran cold. I thought next time I need to simply shut up and not make a connection; sometimes it just works way too well.

But that's not why he was on his knees. He had done something in Wichita that he needed to ask my forgiveness for. It was something that was bothering him so much that he had to come out and apologize in person. It was *nothing* that I had been aware of, let alone bothered by. Even after he told me, I was more than willing to let it go.

What amazed me was that he would go to such lengths to apologize.

Of course I forgave him. There was nothing, in my mind, to forgive. But we worked it through until he felt better. And I was given a moment of being intrinsically valued, as simply another human being. By someone with a huge amount of honor and respect and integrity.

It was not a relationship that would ever work. We knew that and didn't even consider it. He was entrenched in Kansas, with kids from his divorce. I couldn't leave California, for the same reason.

He was a pilot, strictly military, Semper Fi, buttoned down and structured. I'm a literary intellectual living mostly in my head. He forced me to defend my politics; he argued his articulately and with passion.

We made no sense—as a couple, as anything long-term, as much of anything.

But we found ourselves in San Pedro the next morning. It was a serene Saturday. A hauntingly transcendent piece of music was playing on my car stereo. We were with his brother, sister-in-law and nephew. I was with people I'd never see again, people from a different world. The sun was shining and a melody was filling the morning with an aching loveliness.

I was utterly happy.

Someone had bothered to do a Great Thing on my behalf.

It made no sense.

We would lose touch over the years. He was from a completely different world. And yet it was a moment of grace.

Moments of grace do not make for great stories. They are too magical and they evaporate when written down. They are gifts. They are untranslatable. And they come at random moments on little cat feet, just when we need them the most.

You had me at 'No'

I *fancy myself a connoisseur* of unavailable men. There's a lot to be said for hooking up with someone who isn't completely there. I can project all sorts of cool patterns upon them without actually getting into the reality thing. I can commit myself fully without really meaning it; and by the rules of the game, they'll never be able to call me on it. With an unavailable man you never have to worry about your own true availability.

S-w-e-e-t.

Unavailability takes all sorts of shapes. Marriage or other serious commitment is kind of an impediment to availability (sometimes even when he's married to you.) Geography can pose a problem—or enhance and prolong excitement, depending on how fast you can type, how many minutes you're willing to put on your cell phone plan, and how much imagination you can bring to the telephone late at night.

Choosing unavailable people is usually unconscious. After every disaster, I tell myself that I'm searching for that person who is truly emotionally (and legally) (and geographically) available. My unfailing radar always hones in on the person with the biggest zing, however, and that person is usually some form of unavailable.

I saw a dinner theatre show once in which a character named Mr. Available comes to the rescue of a New Age woman. She is seeking someone to share her life with amongst the co-dependent commitment-phobic in-touch-with-their-feminine-side-but-male-empowered New Age men of her demographic. Along comes Mr. Available who is neither married nor insensitive nor living on the wrong coast.

Everything is fine until she pulls out the one thing that can bring Mr. Available to his knees: a diamond. He wavers in pain, waffling between being Mr. Available to her and renouncing his ability to be Mr. Available to anyone else. And thus his downfall: any time a man becomes attached to one woman he is, by definition, unable to become attached to anyone else. The thought drives him berserk.

Emotional unavailability is really my specialty. It's not always apparent right off the bat. Sometimes the guy's brain starts kicking in shortly after the first few bouts of great sex and he starts coming up with a list of "valid" reasons for why the relationship cannot continue.

Sometimes he'll start cringing at certain words, such as "exclusivity." I've become so used to the unavailable man that now, when I meet someone who is emotionally available (to the extent that any sentient human can be), I immediately become the one who cringes at the words and starts screening the calls.

Hitting that wall of emotional distance is like finding out that the other person actually lives in Antarctica. And, as it turns out, is not at all interested in moving. This turns me on. I love a good puzzle and I don't mind a challenge.

Once sucked into the game, I find myself embarking on a trip to visit him in his frozen wasteland. I find the perfect emotional mukluks that will enable me to join him in his territory—only to find out (once I've arrived) that he actually lives in Brazil. Now even more intrigued, I then chase him around the emotional globe, never finding myself in the same place that he is ever again.

Of course it works both ways. I can change emotional citizenship a dozen times myself in one night if I feel threatened. Once someone starts closing in on my vulnerability, I pull out more changes of identity than a KGB operative.

The question is really about who is available here. Perhaps I've refined my gift for finding the unavailable man so I can relax my own defenses for a while. If I start hanging out with someone who is *there*, what would that mean for me? I would either have to spend a great deal of energy keeping my walls solidly fortified, or (God forbid) I'd have to start delving into some deep, uncomfortable levels. I would have to lift up rocks and find bugs underneath that I would prefer to hide for the next fifty years. I would have to be the one who avoids The Talks. Or, worse, I'd actually have to *have* the talks.

Ewwwwww. Icky.

If someone were there I would have to be vulnerable. I would have to answer for my passionate unpredictable heart.

There's a perversity at work here. If someone is lucky enough to get in past my formidable defenses, I start dancing like crazy to keep my perimeters covered. If someone is not so lucky, more often than not I start dancing like crazy just to keep him from dumping me. Because being dumped feels bad, no matter who is doing it.

Either way, it seems I'm doing a lot of dancing. Dancing to keep safe, dancing to seduce, dancing inevitably to just keep dancing.

So *am* I available? No. Of course not.

It seems that no one is available, at least in the sense that very few people willingly and spontaneously open up completely. Thank God sex feels good or else these emotional land mines would've killed off the species millennia ago.

How to proceed? Obviously it's not a good idea to get in deep with everyone we meet. Unavailability, conscious or otherwise, is our way of keeping safe. And safety is fundamentally a good thing. It's only a problem when the things we do to keep safe keep us from living fully. It's when the fences entrap us that they become troublesome.

If we think of these fences of unavailability as useful, we might have the beginnings of a decent model with which to work our way out of this mess. If a fence is hindering our freedom (and we have the courage to recognize it), maybe we can leave it alone to slowly deteriorate. However, a fence that is keeping us secure can be mended and kept in place. Good fences make good neighbors; too many fences make for a lonely life.

We need to know when it's safe to bring down a fence. We need to know when it will work and when it won't. I think it boils down to one of those deceptively simple equations: if both parties so desire, maybe they can embark on a path where availability is a mutual goal. In time you will open your soul up to me, and I to you. Our connection will go subterranean and no fences will be needed at all. We can then build our fences around both of us rather than between us. And we will build a place where we can be safe from the outside as well as safe with each other.

First Impressions

I *wasn't going to show up*, I hated everything, I only wanted to come back home and get some work done.

I procrastinated getting dressed and, on the way up to the meeting place, I left about a dozen voice mails on my girlfriend's cell phone: I hated men, I hated her, I hated first dates, I hated sex.

I have a rich full life. Why do I want to muck it up with a guy? Why am I *going* through all this? Honestly, I just don't know.

I have an endless supply of fantasies about what it would be like to have a great mate. But my fantasies include having enough time and money, too. As long as I'm dreaming, I'll dream about the perfect man *and* the getaway villa in Nice *and* a body that looks like Kate Hudson's.

But I don't regularly go to open houses on the French Riviera, hoping that if I visit enough I'll be able to afford one. Nor do I periodically try on size 3 jeans just to see if they will fit. Why this constant testing of the relationship waters to see if this person is *it*?

There are known procedures for acquiring villas and perfect bodies. Few of them are fun, but all of them have a chance of working. To get a villa you must have money. You steal it, inherit it, find it, earn it or borrow it. It's not easy, but it's straightforward.

Same with a perfect body. If you want to spend money enough and time, it's achievable. Not a pleasant process, but the guidelines are in place.

But how to find the perfect mate? Unknown. Who the hell knows how it's done? The ones that seem like they should be appropriate are wildly out of whack in reality, while the ones you'd never believe possible suddenly click and you're riding high for a week, a month, a year. Is there a way to quantify all this?

It's more like a gamble than any kind of business venture. You can go for years and not make any hits or you can have one jackpot after another, coming so fast upon the heels of the last that you can barely stuff your pockets fast enough with all the winnings.

These days, I feel like I'm stuffing the slot machines with coins, waiting for the next big win. I haven't heard emotional payola setting off bells in a long time. My love affair these days is with the women I work with, my writing partner, my fellow mothers. That's where I start hearing the jingle of soul currency falling into the tray.

Whenever I share a belly laugh with any of them—which is blissfully and fabulously often—I feel a completely new type of endorphin rush. It's different from a sexual love. It's a kind of awakening to the world—a momentary flash of color in the midst of the usual grays of daily life. It's true and it's refreshingly different from the dating game I'm currently playing with the men in my life.

First impressions. What must this man think about me? Too high octane? Too high maintenance? Too smart, too neurotic, too … much? I fear all that is the case. But I'm not going to tone it down just to grab someone who can't handle it. What is the point in that?

So I wait until I find someone who can hook in, hang on, and hold out long enough to get all of it. Long enough to appreciate it. Long enough not to be scared. And long enough to actually relax in all of this with me. Long enough to entrain—to match pendulum swings with me, to breathe with me at night in steady, unself-conscious rhythms.

I'm looking for someone who will stick around long enough to become a partner in sleep and a co-conspirator in life. Someone who can go the distance a little bit further than most, who dares to get it, who has stuff of his own to bring to the table.

I don't know if I've already met this person or not. Perhaps, if I already know him, he has not yet come forward and embraced the potential between us. Or maybe we know the potential all too well, and haven't been able to negotiate the rapids well enough to end up on the same shore yet.

But we will see. The river flows forward and all our paddling and analyzing can't do much to change any part of it. So all we can do is keep looking, breathlessly, and try to enjoy the journey.

The *Poof!* Factor

My parents split up when I was in early elementary school. After that, I only connected sporadically with my dad. We would meet, it'd be great, then he would get outrageously aggrieved about something and cast me out of his life forever.

Years would go by. We'd connect again. Two or three outings later, *poof!* and that was that. Turns out he was actually pissed at my mom, but of course I thought the problems were with me and I did a beautiful job of internalizing all of it.

I instigated what I assumed would be a final meeting with my dad when I was in my early 20s. That one "took" and we had a close relationship until his death 20 years later. Finally, I had met someone of my own species. Even though we got off to a terrible start, we made it up on the back end.

Eventually, of course, there was the final *poof!* Our last two-sided conversation ended with a fight, a situation I was afraid would happen every time we hung up on each other with nasty words still lingering in the air. However, it was a fight with tremendous love as underpinnings, and I fault neither of us for the cranky and inevitable last set of words.

So, that's how it works with most of the men in my life. *Poof!* I connect and rejoice in finding a member of my own species. Then, *poof!* it ends. Sometimes it ends quickly, and most of the time it ends with a great deal of love still intact. Still, I find myself hungering for the connection that was so intermittently available to me. And it's in search of that connection that I live my life.

That's the version of the *Poof!* facor that's easiest to talk about, mainly because I don't have to take any responsibility for anything. It puts the blame squarely on my dad and the metaphysics of my early childhood, playing the same patterns over and over.

But there's another version. One that's harder for me to admit.

I am defiantly independent. I've been on my own since 18. I worked my way through college. One reason I think my marriage lasted as long as it did was that I was adamant about earning my half of the income and doing (at least) my share of the work, and Tom was more than happy to let me.

I've realized recently that this independence has a growl inside of it. I don't like people telling me what to do, or how to live my life. Perhaps this is a legacy of my childhood, but I don't trust easily and I don't particularly see a need to be dependent on anyone.

Never have. Never will.

Maybe the *Poof!* thing is not the universe playing out the same stories for me. Maybe it has something to do with me growling out my independence and the other party finally listening and saying, Man, I'm *outa* here.

There's a downside to all this. We've been having these amazing rainstorms here in Southern California this year. One of them was pummeling the house as I was working on an early draft of this book. I am in a good relationship at the moment, and we allow each other lots of space. So I was alone that night and feeling warm, independent and complete.

I had just closed up my laptop. I was pleased with the work I had done and the rain outside made everything cozy.

My children were snuggled up in their beds in the next room, and my heating system no longer whistled every time it kicked in because I'd been a Conscientious Homeowner and changed the filter for the first time ever. A gusty cross breeze from the storm came in through the windows. I snuggled under the covers, and burrowed in like a little animal in its nest.

I needed nothing and nobody. I was utterly and sublimely content.

Swirling to sleep on this buoyant wave of serenity, I think I hear a crack of a floorboard. I'm instantly awake: maybe Jack is creeping down from the top bunk to come and snuggle with me. But no … nothing else.

I burrow back in. My thoughts start forming into dreams. I settle in like I'm waiting for a movie to start … and I hear another crack.

Before I can even rouse myself, I hear a ripping and then a soft huge bunching type of falling peeling detaching crashing sound. What the hell … ? I sit up. The rain is falling harder. And there definitely is something out there that had detached from something else.

I get up and peer out the window and see some darkness that may not have been there before.

I walk to the next room. Sure enough, I see it out my office windows. It's pressed up, hard, against my kitchen windows and door. I have a branch the size of a yacht taking up my entire back patio and hillside. My kitchen feels like it's underwater. Dripping leaves and branches are pressed against all the windows.

Whoa.

I'm not scared. But …

Whoa.

I don't know exactly what to do. I don't particularly

want to go outside and see what's going on. I figure if it'd gone through the roof, I'd know it. But would I? This is precisely the first time I've had a huge amount of tree fall down on top of my house in the middle of the night.

So I call my boyfriend. The boyfriend I was so happy to be independent from just twenty minutes before. The boyfriend whose place in bed I had replaced with my laptop. The boyfriend who respects my boundaries and need for space and who tries to understand when I just want to be alone. I call him.

Why?

Because as much as I completely hate to admit it, on that dark and stormy night I was a woman and I needed a man. It was as simple as that.

After talking to him for a few minutes, I feel brave enough to go outside and battle the drippy mess. It is true: A huge chunk of tree is now very much in my life. Then I come back in, dry off, and call him back. He offers to come over but I say no. There isn't anything he can *do*. But he wanted to come and be used as a buffer between the elements and me.

And as I went to sleep with the wind still blowing and the rain still pouring I finally understood something. As much as I would like to be a little self-sufficient island, I'm simply not. I have needs for the warmth and protection that only other people can provide, and other people need qualities that can uniquely come from me—as a mother, as a writer, as a friend. When the trees come through the roof, we need warmth and a sense of being partnered with other humans against the wild unpredictable storms of the world.

Even though I didn't need this man to come over just to protect me from more branches, I was glad he was around for this one. And the next day, when he came over and walked around my roof checking for damage, I was deeply moved. *Poof!* there he was, walking on the roof, doing what he could to take care of me.

And I realized that sometimes, many times, people can *Poof! into* your life as well.

Crossing the Great Water

Take a moment to seriously appreciate your kidneys. Kidneys are *very* important. Until recently, I had never thought about kidneys for a second. But, as I'm finding out, they are there for a purpose. As is everything else.

My father is dying. And I'm learning a lot. The body's systems are incredibly mysterious and complex. The poetry between the interchanges of functions and design is mystically beautiful. There is something far beyond the sum of the parts going on. And while I have to admit I know nothing about human physiology, I have to acknowledge the sophistication of the design team that evolved this particular piece of software. The human body is quite a piece of code.

I had a wonderful opportunity to talk to a nurse during my vigil in the intensive care unit with my dad. I was fascinated by the fact that she gets to see life and death at such close hand on a daily basis. From talking to her I learned she's been working bedside for 20 years. She has passed up opportunities to rise up to management or move away from the ICU unit.

Here are some of the things she told me.

She wouldn't trade her job "for love or money," a direct quote. That alone stopped me in my tracks. Most of us earn far more money than this woman. We never get blood or urine (or worse) on our hands. We reside in the safe buffer zone of mental battlegrounds, rather than on the actual borderline between life and death. We go through our routines with varying degrees of detachment, anger and boredom. Sometimes we're enthusiastic. But how many of us would say: "I wouldn't trade my job for love or money"?

Think about that.

Of course it is very hard, she said. People in her line of work respond in several ways. You can wall yourself off, detach yourself and then go home and forget about it. Or you can use it to connect. That's what she does. She is impassioned because it connects her to the true fundamentals. It keeps everything in perspective. It's a mainline to the things that count.

There are many ways to die, she has observed. There are difficult deaths and there are easy deaths. Death is an obvious thing. Even if the body is still being artificially maintained, there is an obvious, clear and significant moment when the transition is made.

It is not physiological. It is spiritual. She says this without a moment's hesitation or an iota of doubt. The difference between an alive body and a dead one is whether or not the spirit is residing within it.

People go when they need to go. Like a pregnancy that cannot be forced to go full term, all the life support measures will not sustain life if it's not meant to be. And, at the same time, people will stay alive, despite horrible odds, as long as it's necessary.

She was sure about this issue of time. All the medicine and intervention in the world does not change this fact. We go when it's time to go. We cannot play God. We cannot choose. All we can do as caregivers is make the traveler comfortable as he goes down his path.

Death is not a bad thing, she said. And it's "not as final as most people think." People continue on in memories and how they've affected and shaped our lives. Their bodies may die, but they don't.

Watching my dad, I think about how important it is to keep the accounts clear in life. Everything we say and do and think affects the nature of how we go and what this moment brings. Part of what determines an easy vs. a difficult death is the degree to which we are holding on. It's not just about our attachment to other people … it's the degree of our attachment to life itself.

It seems that the amount of lingering is proportional to the amount of internal reckoning one has to do. My dad has been hanging on for almost a week. To me, it feels as though he is clearing the decks and stocking the galley prior to pulling away from the dock and starting the long sail across the great waters. While below decks, I feel him doing a large internal audit. Cleaning out the involvements, straightening the books. Whatever is going on inside his unconscious body is very deep and focused work.

The degree to which we've kept our vessel in shape and accounts in order is, perhaps, indicative of how easy that setting forth will be.

These thoughts are not meant to bum anyone out. Quite the contrary. What all this indicates to me is that the concerns surrounding our daily jobs, our relationships, our children, and our lives are *very* real concerns and truly stressful. After spending some time on the frontier between the living and dying, I have come to see our daily battles as wonderfully life-affirming.

The engagement in the human dance is what it's all about. We are born, we form communities and families, we interact. We fight and we love and we care for each other. There are long solitary nighttime vigils for every one of us, at one time or another. There are moments of intense joy and laughter even beside the deathbeds of loved ones. There is no possible way to figure it all out. But the dance is the thing. Even when it's stupid. Even when it's futile. Good, bad, indifferent—all roads lead to that ultimate moment of preparing the ship for the final sail.

Waystation

O*n the last conscious day* of my father's life he went to the local Ralph's supermarket and bought two bottles of Wishbone salad dressing, two bags of iceberg lettuce, two boxes of Cubbison's croutons and a 48-ounce bottle of Coors. He came home and sat in his favorite chair in the living room of his small apartment, munching on salad and downing the beer. He carefully closed up the opened bag of croutons with a paper clip.

We don't know what happened. But at some point he vomited. At another point he carefully placed his teeth in the bathroom sink. He was wearing his leather coat. He had been getting very cold at night lately, even though we were well into spring and entering a toasty Southern California summer.

We found him three and a half days later, naked and barely conscious, on the floor. He had lived for probably 86 hours without moving, excreting or probably very much blood pressure, sustained only by salad and beer. He was one tough old guy. He was 90.

I didn't know him until he was 70. I was 23 and figured he was going to kick any minute and didn't want him to become a psychological monster in my head. I wanted to do battle with him, make him pay for all the hurt he inflicted on me since the time he left my mother when I was about seven. A few times in those intervening years we had tried to have a relationship; each time ended up with his tyrannical anger and my mothers' tight-lipped tension whenever anything regarding my father would be mentioned. I didn't understand it had nothing to do with me.

The night before we met again, when I was 23, I was terrified. I was sure he was going to kill me—emotionally, psychologically, somehow. I vowed that I would never, ever tell him I loved him, like I did when I was a vulnerable little kid. I would never open up and let him get close enough to strike a killing blow. I carried all my tough little vows with me to that first meeting. But we met, we talked and we watched sailboats together. And I realized, whether I liked it or not, that we were of the same species.

I have very few memories of him from when I was little. The most distinct one I have is of crouching on the other side of the bathroom door while he was inside conducting his morning business. I was maybe three years old. He'd be seated and I'd scribble little notes to him and slip them under. I remember convulsing with glee over this. My mother thought it was improper. My dad and I loved it.

Our visitation periods never lasted longer than four months. During one of these times, he outfitted his blue VW van with curtains and a bed for me in the back, in case I got sleepy. Then he took me on a little road trip up to Hearst Castle, where we marveled at the magnificent gaudiness of the estate. We were of the same species that day, too.

People who knew my father in his prime remember him as a very successful man. He had been in the shoe business, starting off as a salesman on Market Street in San Francisco just after the Depression began to thaw. He was a hearty partaker of the pleasures of the Barbary Coast, getting his jaw broken once after some misplaced comment (he was good at those). He was devilishly good-looking; a picture I have from 1934 shows a dark-eyed dandy with slicked-back hair, staring out at the world with a rakish confidence hovering just beneath the surface. The women loved him.

And he loved back. He understood women deeply, which was why he was such a success in the shoe business. After he had become a buyer at Ransohoff's, he designed a line of black pumps, each with a different lining of brightly colored Thai silk. The colors were saturated and sensuous—violet, turquoise, teal, vermilion—yet completely hidden to the outside world. "The girls walked with a little extra bounce, knowing they had something special going on," he'd chuckle with retailer's glee. "The shoes just flew off the shelves."

His second wife was a window-dresser at Gump's; she was petite, artistic and wild. They spent most of their pre-war years intoxicated, tearing up and down the hills of their beloved San Francisco in a bright yellow Hudson convertible. Family legend has it that the famous *San Francisco Chronicle* columnist, Herb Caen, mentioned their marriage in his column.

Every waitress, every woman on the bus was instantly noticed and assessed (sometimes none too favorably). Even shuffling along at 90, he'd peer up at a passing nurse and say with complete sincerity "You look *wonderful* today," and they would melt. Once he took the shoe off one of my girlfriend's feet to examine it. "He made me feel like Cinderella," she wrote in her condolence card to me. When he felt like it, he made every girl feel like Cinderella.

He had a rare and marvelous eye for appreciating the small details of life. He loved every nuance of weather. He relished disasters—earthquakes in particular. A Caesar salad and a steak barbecued on a hibachi while moored at Avalon was his idea of heaven. And he loved his wine. He found the cheap stuff as delectable as the fancy, and he'd defend it staunchly, making up stories about the vintage and the baron who bottled it in his estate on the Rhine. It was an act of romance to unscrew the top of each bottle and indulge in a glass (or three). He relished anything that could have a story attached.

But there was a dark side to all the story-weaving. Danger lurked in every corner. The bastards were *always* out to get him. Life was a hostile territory that you had to battle through or be killed in the process. He was the original hippie: all authority enraged him, taunted him, made him put up his dukes. He fought all of them for years, quitting his job because "they just didn't understand." His businesses went under. His multiple inventions failed. No one understood. And there was always a story why.

When the bastards quit being an actual impediment, he started looking under rocks, manufacturing scenarios. His savings depleted, his stock ventures gone awry, he found himself living on Social Security and decided to take on the government itself. He spent the last ten years of his life concocting elaborate conspiracy scenarios and trying to get back his money from the elected officials who had done him wrong.

He always pushed back. And he always pushed forward. There wasn't a tunnel too foreboding to explore, no sail too risky to undertake, no cliff too steep to climb. As he got older his adventures became more and more outrageous. He could never stop and say "OK, today I'll take it easy." When the adventures turned bad and he was cut and bleeding, he pressed on. "Why should I have turned back, Kathy?" he said to me once in the ER. "I'd already been there."

Looking back on the past few years, I realize that there were many signs of his weakening heart. His coldness at night. His inability to remember nouns with any kind of accuracy. Mounting paranoia and anger. A hunched, lopsided gait. His extremities just must not have been getting very well nourished, including his poor fierce brain.

My last (two-sided) conversation with him was a fight. He wanted me to drop everything one night and go to Glendale, about 15 miles away, to buy him a television set that was on sale at the K-Mart. I offered to call it in with a credit card but he said no. I offered to take him the next day. Nope. He didn't want to do it that way. He was angry and so tired of everything being difficult.

He told me he was going to have a couple of drinks, and that would solve everything. He hung up, angry and frustrated. And the next day he went to get some salad fixings and a big tall beer. I didn't thaw out from my own annoyance for about four days, when he missed our weekly lunch date. He went out pissed, and on his own terms.

Even when I wasn't in the hospital, my entire spirit was residing in the room with the hissing, sighing ventilator, the monitors with the seismic graphs, the still, tubed form wrapped in white on the bed. His nurses and doctors were beautiful women all. (I know he was deeply pleased.) Together we made decisions about his kidneys, pain relief and life support.

After four days, the losses were outstripping the gains. Finally we agreed to increase the morphine and let the consequential drop in blood pressure do what it needed to do. We didn't pull any plugs, but we decided not to add any more either.

I took a deep breath and sat by my father's bedside, fortified with a red pen and some editing I'd brought with me to do. The nurse dimmed the lights. She turned off the sounds of the monitors. Alarms weren't all that necessary any more. I settled down and tried to work, desperately trying to pretend this wasn't happening. Beside me the ventilator breathed in and out.

Finally I stopped. I'd been watching the blood pressure monitor far more often than I was reading my pages. And I realized that this situation only happens once (thankfully), but it needed to be attended to, as much as I could bear.

His hands and feet were blue, almost frost-bitten by the lack of circulation. I touched his hand gently, around the IV and the tape. The ventilator hissed, slowed down, hissed, slowed. The blood pressure dropped. Stabilized. Then dropped some more.

My father's favorite time of year was the end of August, when the huge thermal clouds bunched up over the San Gabriels, gloriously white against the hot blue summer sky. He'd watch those clouds as he sailed back from Catalina. There was always one weekend that the clouds were just right and every summer we'd remark on it. It was the Sailing Home From Catalina weekend.

The last morning of his life I realized what these last days in the hospital had felt like. He was moving into his boat. Stowing things below decks, finalizing the ledgers, settling accounts. He was getting ready for a long voyage, thinking things through—both about the journey he'd just completed and the one upon which he was about to embark. I had been hoping that he'd come back up from below long enough to say good-bye, but that wasn't going to happen. He was waiting and working and was finally ready to go.

I touched his cold hand and whispered "Push off, Daddy—I'll throw you the lines." And about 20 seconds later the blood pressure went to zero and he was freed from the dock, floating off slowly and heading out across the great water.

Walking through the halls of the hospital after his death I felt a profound exhaustion, so deep and spiritual and bone-numbing, I remembered only one other time I'd felt anything similar. That was after I'd had my first son, Chris, and was exquisitely tired. I had given birth, and now I had given death.

In the weeks and months after his death, I felt like Charon, the mythological ferryman, who spends his life shuttling people to the shores of Hades, his domain the dark mysterious river between both. I was disenfranchised from both worlds, unable to access wherever it is my father now resides.

And once again, I find myself on the other side of the door from him, scribbling notes across the great divide, hoping that somehow he'll receive them.

Owners of the Dream

I made a small pilgrimage to my old house tonight for my ex-husband's 40th birthday. It's warm and filled with my old friends, his new friends, the friends who took sides, and the few friends who managed to stay true to both of us. I look at the still-empty walls where my furniture used to be.

Women I've never met come up to me and look at me with a weird kind of curiosity. I say, "Hi, I'm Kathy," and they look at me with a smile that says "DUH." Suddenly it registers: I'm not a person named Kathy, I'm the "ex." I could be the Poet Laureate outside this party, but here in my old house I am only that one thing.

I look back at them and think, "You've been with the father of my kids. You've been with him in this house that I poured so much heart and soul and care into for so many years. This warm little home with its Christmas tree and my abandoned wreath on the front door. You slept in my bed."

The jealousy bypasses the man and goes directly to the dream. Someone now is the owner of that dream. Someone now snuggles in that bed and feels that sense of secure peace that I had believed to be mine.

I understand how she feels. It was a nice dream I dreamt in this house. I would've loved to stay in it forever, but I happened to be the one who woke up first. I was the one who forced the questions out into the open. I was the one whose disillusion raged inside the house until the windows shook.

I regret none of it. The awakening had to take place. It was as inevitable as the dawn. And I've spent many hours wondering if it could have worked out otherwise. What if we had *both* awakened and *both* had wanted to create some new dreams together? What if we both could have lived a waking dream—partners in spirit and soul and reality? That would have been glorious. That, above all, would have made for the sweetest story possible.

I look around and wonder if one of these women will wake up in my old bed someday and wonder what happens next. What choices will *she* make? Or maybe he'll wake while she's still asleep. In those moments of first awakening will he somehow suddenly understand what went through my mind so many years before? Maybe he'll know how much better it is when both people are at once awake and in that dream. Maybe he'll figure out that this is the true goal of all of this.

I think that it is the nature of all dreams to fade into reality and become made new, over and over again. If so, I embrace the next awakening. And I look forward to the next dream that I will someday, inevitably, be graced with again.

Odysseus' Storytime

I*'ve been reading Chris and Jack* an adaptation of The Odyssey before bedtime recently. When you get past the fact that this is a story you *had* to read in college and you *had* to understand in order to begin to fathom Joyce's *Ulysses* ... when you get past the fact that it's old and the names are hard to pronounce—damn! It's a great yarn.

The kids think Odysseus is rude and his men are stupid. I agree. More accurately, Odysseus starts *off* rude and seems to learn a few things as he goes on. The men, of course, end up pretty dead. The kids love all their pranks and ruses to get out of trouble. It's gory and scary and nerve-wracking. Just the kind of thing that makes for a good bedtime discussion.

The Gods have their fingers in everything and they argue amongst themselves about how to deal with this poor guy. They change their minds. They play tricks for their own amusement. Sometimes it takes a God going on vacation to get anything to work right.

As I read, I think about how we all must travel through many adventures, tormented by the conflicting whims of the Gods, in order to regain a state of comfort and love lost long ago. How the road to the mythical Ithaca is never clear, never easy, never short.

I find it interesting that most of Odysseus' later adventures seem to involve women and the various ways the heart can be ensnared and kept from finding its way back to its rightful abode. Sometimes we must lash ourselves to the mast to avoid being seduced by the siren's song of deadly beauty. Sometimes only the intervention of the Gods can keep us from becoming a pig like the rest of our companions.

I love Calypso. She was beautiful, kind, and took good care of Ulysses. He lived with her for nine years. One assumes they were perfectly happy, except for the fact that he'd go off every day and stare off at the sea, longing with tears on his face for the home he'd lost. Everything was OK enough, except for the fact that it was not Ithaca, she was not Penelope, it was not home.

Poor sad Odysseus. How I understand your lonely wanderings. Yet your adventures were lovely. And important. The Gods had their reasons for causing you to take this route.

I wonder, what happens next? When you get back

home to Ithaca, and finally cradle your beloved Penelope in your arms ... what do *you* think about as you're going to sleep? Do you think back on the land of the lotus-eaters and the island of the Cyclops and grin to yourself in the dark, savoring your cleverness in getting away? Do you think of your dinners with Circe and wonder how she's doing these days? Did you ever write a quick note to dear Calypso, thanking her for those nine years of putting up with your restless soul?

What bedtime stories do you tell your grandchildren, Odysseus? Do you always end the story with the comforting assurance that one always, eventually, comes home to rest? Or do you trail off as they fall asleep, letting the adventures linger and dissipate as you sit alone in the dark?

I see you spinning the stories differently from night to night. Sometimes you're the hero. Sometimes you're the butt of those prankster Gods' jokes. Sometimes it's about the longing to be back on this very island. Sometimes it's being reunited with your family, rightfully connected.

But the stories you do not tell are always in the back of your mind. The smell of the sea haunts you; the memories of the narrow escapes make you smile to yourself. I see you sitting in the dark, Odysseus, humming the siren's song to yourself and feeling the aching mixture of yearning and joy.

Acknowledgements

In a life filled with children, work, people and responsibilities, the burning drive to write life down and make sense of it all has too often been forced to wait. The true grace in these notes has been in finding enough 15-minute snippets of time to connect the words to form this book, like stringing painfully-harvested pearls of time to form a necklace.

In forcing this book into being, I have had to call in a great many favors and impose my needs upon a great many people. I have dislodged schedules, forgotten appointments and been pretty unpleasant to live with. It has not been a graceful process.

My deepest thanks go out to everyone who has helped me, supported me, encouraged and put up with me throughout this incredible voyage:

To Mara, the shining angel in my life—together we have talked our lives and art into existence, fully visible, glorious and magnificent. Our lives are truly brilliant.

To Cynthia, my light and my muse. Brilliant and with a laugh that comes straight from the soul, your wisdom, perverse humor and dogged tenacity saw this project to completion and beyond.

To Scott, who built me an incredible stage upon which to take my first solo bow. War buddy, truth teller, music weaver, keeper of my sanity. 25 years is not nearly enough time to have been your friend so you're stuck with me for the duration.

To Bridget, there at the very beginning and a tireless advocate and inspiration throughout. Your passion for the book carried me through many dark hours. Thank you for giving so fully of yourself ... in every way!

To Dorthea, ruthless advocate of accuracy, precision and truth. Your editing has made the raw gem glitter and shine.

To Skye, sparkling and incisive, thank you for lovingly and laughingly sharing your glorious vision with all of us.

To Faye, angel of mercy. Appearing out of nowhere, you became one of my most trusted allies and advocates. One thousand respect gestures to you, my friend.

To Cindy, glorious creator and wild woman. You validate my existence as an artist and make me laugh about the insanity of it all. Your work raises the bar to an impossibly high level for all who see it; I am so very proud to be your friend.

And finally to my sisters in RMS—Steph, Val, Melinda and Noelle—you keep me as sane as possible, which is saying a lot (as you know)! With you I get to experience the joys of sisterhood with only some of the occasional struggles. I am so very blessed to have each of you in my daily life.

All of you, you da BAND, man. It is not me in the spotlight, it is all of us up on stage. For once in my life I wish I really *was* a performer so I could turn and introduce you to everyone in person. I could not have done it without you.

Other people in my life have been staunch supporters and must be thanked.

To Michael, my companion, friend and lover of the last two years. Your steadfast tenacity has been instrumental in enabling me to write this book. Thank you for being there, for working through the tough places, for always coming from a place of growth and caring. May your bright inner light continue to sparkle and grow.

Tom, partner in life, no matter how separate our mailboxes. I cherish your brilliance and your soul and your deep inherent goodness. May our sense of humor never fade and may our children flourish within all of our embraces.

Keith: Jack says you're like his Game Boy—disappearing for long periods of time and then showing up when least expected. You woke me up and started me on this journey; despite the detours and long silences, a part of me is still sitting on your back deck, drinking merlot out of a jam glass and listening to crickets in the night. My conversation is always with you.

To my mother, who has taught me the wisdom of taking the high road and how to handle difficulty with compassion. You always urged me to do what I love; this book is the hard-won result.

To Jane Murphy, shaman, sister and guide through fast waters; I could not have done it without your wisdom and compassion. I am deeply grateful for all the time we've shared.

To Guro El, Black Swan, maiden warrior extraordinaire, thank you for the constant mainline of energy and passion, inspiration and grace. Your rhythms tap into the beating of all our hearts.

To Arlene, fierce warrior princess. You have stood at my side and kept me protected with your green healing light. Infinite respects, my dear friend.

To the rest of my tribe at Magda Institute, you are my family, my people, and the whetstone upon which I sharpen my sword. I thank you all for your passion and dedication to the art; it humbles and inspires me.

To all my other Soul Sistahs—Jill D., Kathy, Jillian, Jasmine, Isabella, Lori, Alexandra, Kate, Debby, Carol, Jill B., LoriAnn, Vivian, Salgal, Kathy Shirek, and Nancy Marie (still and always)—my conversations with you over the years have taught me so much about being a woman, a mother and a fellow voyager. If there's a heaven, we will all meet up and have an eternity of pajama parties together.

To all the people mentioned in these pages, I thank you humbly for being part of my life, for changing me, for making me think and feel. These are stories about my reality—situations have been skewed to better serve that story, not to chronicle precise events. If I have changed things to preserve my own truth at the expense of the accuracy of the situation, I claim artistic license and beg your indulgence. No dishonor was in any way intended. Quite the contrary.

To those I did not mention: You know you are loved, and why you did not make it into these stories. Some stories are as big as the patterns in the clouds, continually changing and reforming.

Most especially, I thank my children. You have amazed, astounded and delighted me since the days you each entered the world. You are handling your journey through this world with grace, profound intelligence and great humor. You are by far the coolest people I have ever known. Thank you for dealing with my cranky days and preoccupied nights and giving me buckets of love and understanding in return. I love you as much as the grains of sand, multiplied by the stars in the sky, times infinity.

Bonus Tracks

Like offbeat relatives, these are essays that have been in my life for years, begging to join the party. They don't exactly fit with the rest of this collection, but they kept knocking on the door and I could not turn them down. I hope you enjoy them as much as I have.

—Kathy

In the Booth

T*he best part of going to a movie* is that moment before the screen bursts open with light. There is the expectant hush, the contented munching of popcorn, the settling in for a short journey away from the real. If it's hot outside, the inside of the theatre is a cool oasis. If it's raining, you gather with other souls in a warm, dry place as primitive as an ancient cave with wall paintings dancing in the firelight. If it's snowing, you know that when you return to reality, the world outside will be subtly changed, just like the world inside has been.

For about six years, in the late seventies and early eighties, I was graced with the ability to provide that moment to hundreds of people on a regular basis. My job as a projectionist enabled me to choose the intermission music (no slide show ads for local car dealerships back then!), dim the lights, open the curtain and flash those first flickering images on the screen.

As I presented a show, I was provided a show in turn. From above, I saw the effete file in for the Godards and the Buñuels. I saw the intellectual hipsters come back for every black-and-white samurai movie (for years all I knew about Kurosawa was that his films were abnormally oily, grimy and invariably broke at least once a showing). At 98 midnight showings of the *Rocky Horror Picture Show* I watched 98 different audiences dress up, dance, squirt squirt guns and toss toasted bread at the screen. I spent a summer of cool matinees at a grand old deco single-screen theatre showing The Empire Strikes Back. I charged from theatre to theatre at one of the few multiplexes in town, galloping up the stairs in darkened theatres on my way to each booth and glancing at the shadowed faces reflecting the light I had shone on the screen for them. Some were laughing. Some had tears.

Getting into the projection biz happened, as fateful things seem to do, very simply. I was a student at U.C. Santa Cruz and had a friend who worked at the candy counter of the Nickelodeon, one of a pair of art houses in town. I hung around mooching free popcorn and movies long enough that I became friendly with the projectionist, Annie. Annie was a smart and determined young woman who was galled by her minority position as the second female projectionist in all the Northern California I.A.T.S.E. unions. When I expressed an interest in seeing the booth and watching her work, she quickly fixated on the idea of gaining another sister in the trade.

The training was arduous. I had to learn a booth and get checked out before being allowed to work a shift. I had to work a certain number of shifts before I was allowed to apply to the union. Once checked out and official, I would work at theatres where the lead projectionist was sick or had a day off and where all the higher-ranking operators were also unavailable or unwilling to work. The more houses I was checked out at, the more likely I was to get work.

I trained several booths and got to know several other projectionists in the trade. Their booths were the expressions of their souls. Many solitary hours spent baby-sitting the machinery, punctuated by 20-minute intervals when a change of reels was required, usually resulted in nests of metaphysical manifestations: their booths mirrored the inner person.

The lead projectionist at the Nickelodeon, Armon, had built a complex network of devices to help him keep his booth running smoothly. He built a crane so that the diminutive Annie would be able to hoist 6000 foot reels up to the huge spindle of an odd duck of a projector, the Cinemeccanica. (The Cinemeccanica itself was a character, an Italian beast as daring as a sports car but as temperamental as an old woman. The Cinemeccanica carried within its design weird manifestations of its makers' world views: the superstitious Italians did not include the number '13' anywhere in the circuitry or mechanics of the projector; form was more important than function in the assumption that the elegance of combining three reels would far override the logistical difficulty of hoisting the huge reel high overhead in order to thread the machine. I've never trusted Italian cars since I worked with that projector.) Armon Armonized the splicing process, fine-tuned the rewind, and kept his machines perfectly oiled and spotlessly maintained.

The projectionist at the Rio Theatre, Harlow Packard, had apparently worked his booth since the beginning of time. He seemed to be close to ninety. He had a chair in the corner, the springs and stuffing and remnants of upholstery alchemically fused and perfectly molded to his form. A stack of newspapers, yellowing at the bottom, was on one side of the chair. A table with a mug stained almost black and a stack of more recent papers was on the other side. He moved from this chair only at the last possible moment to change the reel, thread up the new machine, and then walk slowly back. He hadn't been able to really see the screen for years, so we younger relief guys tweaked the focus for him on our shifts. He would tell stories in a rusty dry voice, about the turntables mounted on the backs of the projector bases, about the Mighty Wurlitzers and nitrate film. He would interject these stories sometimes with a sigh and say, "And then came *sound*," like it had all been pretty much downhill from there.

I eventually settled down at the Nickelodeon's sister art house, the Sash Mill Cinema. It was a sweet gig. There was a café downstairs, all my friends regularly attended the independent films that changed two or three times a week, and the projectionists could choose some pretty cool and eclectic intermission music. The lead projectionist there had great taste and I discovered some lifelong passions in the music he had available. I played Keith Jarrett before most of the movies, *Let it Bleed* before the *Rocky Horror Picture Show*, and had a particular fondness for Albinoni's *Adagio in G Minor*, a piece so melancholy that my friends begged me to stop playing it as it thoroughly bummed them out before the movie even started.

Besides learning about how all the machines worked and having a fundamental knowledge of how to fix simple disasters, the most exacting maneuver I had to learn was how to execute a changeover. Each booth contained two projectors, each of which would run a 20-minute reel. The skill, the artistry and the heady challenge of the job consisted of seamlessly changing from one machine to the other so that the moviegoers never noticed the change.

Most films required five or six such changeovers. Longer ones would have ten or even 12 reels. No matter how long I worked or how comfortable I was with the equipment, changeovers always provided me with a good shot of adrenaline.

All projectors are equipped with the same basic equipment: a light source, a projector head through which the film travels, and a sound head which reads the soundtrack and broadcasts the sound through speakers in the house. For a changeover to work, the film, sound, motor and light systems for both projectors must sync up long enough for the projectionist to seamlessly change the projection from one machine to the other.

I most frequently used a carbon arc lamp house for the light source. In these lamp houses two carbon rods about the size of a pencil are mounted with their tips pointing at each other like accusatory fingers. Each rod is charged with a high current of opposing electrical current—when you touch them together briefly the rods arc, just like touching a jumper cable to a battery node.

The trick is to capture that arc and nurse it so that it produces a very bright sustainable light. If the rods are too far apart, the ball of flame will dim and die. If the rods are too close together, the rods burn too brightly and can eventually fuse. (I don't know what exactly happens after that, but my impression is that it is similar to crossing the streams in the Ghostbusters devices: the end of the civilized world as we know it or something hideously equivalent.) When properly controlled the carbon arc light is intense, beautiful and produces a light similar in quality to that of the sun.

The projector head is a motorized system that moves the film from a full reel, through a film gate containing a device called an intermittent movement, down to the sound head, and then to a take-up reel. The countdown leader at the head of a reel of film is actually there for the projectionist, not just because it looks cool when it mistakenly gets shown on the screen. Eight is the magic number, the number to align in the framing aperture. Once the machine starts running, it'll take eight seconds of getting up to speed and running smoothly before the first frame of the movie appears. Eight seconds is also the amount of time between the cue marks at the end of a reel of film.

The intermittent movement inside the projector head is a thing of mechanical elegance that pulls the film, stops it for ¹⁄₂₄th of a second in front of the open aperture of light, and then moves it on. The way our brains are wired, we need to see an image stop for a fraction before we can successfully link it to the next image in our heads. This "persistence of vision" takes a series of discrete images and creates smooth movement. If we didn't have a moment to capture that image in our brains, all we'd see is a blur.

When threading up, the projectionist needs to make sure the intermittent movement is stopped at the beginning of a cycle, so that the film stays framed correctly and the line between each frame remains invisible. To frame it up correctly, I used my fingers to feel the teeth on the pull-down roller beneath the gate while hand-cranking the motor. My fingers always smelled of machine oil.

We used optical sound heads back then in the days before digital ("*and then there was sound!*"), which read squiggly white lines printed off to the side of each frame to produce sound. Much like the needles of old turntables 'read' the grooves on vinyl records, the sound head uses an "exciter lamp" to shine a beam at the soundtrack and translate it to analog sound. The film must be threaded with the correct number of frames between the soundtrack and the frame in the aperture, so the actors' lips stay in sync when they speak.

My cue to start getting nervous (if I wasn't already) was a bell that started ringing on the hub of the running machine. This bell is calibrated to ring as the hub starts moving at a certain speed; the lead projectionist of the booth sets how many seconds there are between the bell and the first of the two changeover cues, so I also learned a lot about an operator by how close they'd cut the timing. Guys like Harlow Packard set it short so they'd have the minimum amount of time between standing up, moving to the machine, starting the lamp house and waiting for the cue mark. Other, less confident, projectionists gave themselves more time to worry and fuss.

At the bell, I turned on the big rectifier in the lamp house, using a huge Frankenstein-like lever to start the juice flowing to the carbon rods. Then I touched the carbons together for a second in order to create the arc. I aligned the carbons so that the light ball was bright, round and correctly balanced between the two rods. To keep the film from frying once the carbons are cranked up, the machine was equipped with a large "hand dowser" that raised and lowered a thick metal plate down in between the lamp house and the projector head. This wouldn't shield out 100% of the light, but it kept enough heat and light out from the projector that the film didn't get too hot and the audience didn't see shadows and light coming from the second projector.

After the lamp house was juiced up, I'd move to the front of the projector and double-check that the film was threaded correctly and that all the sprockets were correctly seated on all the rollers within the head of the projector. Then I'd peer out of the little window beside the projector, stare at the top right corner of the screen—and wait. What I was looking for were the little round circles printed at the top upper right corner of the frame at the end of every reel, eight seconds apart. (Once you start seeing them it's hard to ever stop, which is at first kind of cool and then extremely annoying.)

This is by far the worst time, waiting for the first cue mark. One hand is on the motor switch to turn on the projector and the other hand is on the hand dowser. If your eyes burn, you can't blink. If you sneeze you'd better hope fervently that you didn't miss the mark. If the other machine makes a funny noise or (God forbid!) the film breaks, you can't do anything about it. It is the emotional equivalent of having to send your opposite-sex child into a restroom in a public place while you wait outside; the need to wait calmly while envisioning a multitude of unpleasant scenarios creates an intense sense of urgency that you can do absolutely nothing about.

If all goes well, you don't miss the first cue mark.

You see the cue and then simultaneously start the motor and raise the hand dowser. The light is blocked by the "electronic dowser" which is electronically linked to the other machine. The film starts moving through the head of the projector, eight seconds away from the first frame.

After the first changeover mark, you're now running two projectors and the need to keep riveted on the screen is even more imperative. Now you have two vulnerable children outside of your control and all you can do is hope that, for the next eight seconds, you don't do anything wrong and nothing happens to them.

The biggest fear is that you missed the first changeover cue and the next thing you (and everyone else in the audience) will see is the end leader flickering through the gate. If this happens, you're screwed. You have three choices: You change to the new machine early and show the countdown leader; you finish counting to eight and hope there's enough end leader on the old machine so that you don't completely embarrass yourself by splashing white light all over the screen; or you trust in The Force and just guess when the best time in the middle will be. If you're extremely lucky, you can make the change before the end of the old reel and after the numbers stop on the new reel. If not, all you can do is hope that the willing suspension of disbelief is particularly strong for the current film. No matter what, you buy yourself some new gray hairs.

If you successfully started the process rolling, you stand peering out the window and try to keep all those scenarios at bay as you stand there and wait for the second cue mark. I always silently counted eight seconds to myself just in case the cue mark was mysteriously gone or I sneezed or blinked or something else went wrong. If all goes well, in eight seconds the film in the new machine advances to the first frame of the picture, the arc has stayed bright and steady and the other projector is smoothly running out of film. When you see the second cue mark, you hit two buttons—one to open the electronic dowser (thus turning off the light in the other machine while simultaneously allowing the light through on the new machine) and one to swap the exciter beam from the old machine to the new one. Voila. Several anxiety attacks later, you've successfully changed to the new reel. And to everyone below, it's just a story moving forward.

After about a year of doing this 100 times or more a week, I started getting used to the impending-train-wreck feeling of the process and really became an adrenaline junkie. Late nights, to keep awake, I'd start picking out the old tossed-out carbons from the coffee cans and play "carbon roulette," putting in the shortest rods I could find to see if they'd last a full twenty minutes. Once I got so immersed in a book that I completely forgot to thread up until the bell started ringing; I had to grab the new reel, thread it and be ready for the changeover in less than a minute. And every so often I'd miss a changeover and I'd get humble and my attention would be pretty good for a few shows longer.

Film breaks are the scariest. I'd be sitting reading

or talking on the phone or just spacing out and suddenly I'd hear something, subliminally, like the sound of an approaching earthquake. All my senses would be instantly on the alert, although I didn't even know why. Sometimes it'd be chatter in the film gate, or a skip in the monotonous drone of the machinery. Sometimes the drone resumed. But when it didn't, or got worse, I'd have to work unbelievably fast.

When a film breaks, it doesn't stop being fed through the rollers so it fills up the projector head very quickly. The film can accordion and crease or, worse, it can slice down the middle so that part of it keeps running through while the other bunches up.

The first thing I'd do is make sure I didn't burn everything up when I'd stop the motor, so I'd throw down the hand dowser and then stop the machine. Unfortunately, everyone in the house can see the disaster as it happens, so instead of watching the blank screen of course they turned to watch *me*. (Luckily the insulation in the booth was usually good enough that I couldn't hear them yelling "Fix the film!!!" "Film break!" Like, duh.)

I'd frantically rip the broken tendrils of film out of the projector head and open up the gates to free them completely. Then, I'd pull down the film to about two feet above where it was broken, reframe the intermittent movement, and thread up, trying to control my shaking hands. I'd wind the broken film up on the takeup reel under the existing film, and mark the place with a piece of paper, to be dealt with later.

Then I'd stand up, take a deep breath, and change

the electronic dowser and sound back to the other, non-running machine. I'd return to the injured soldier, start the motor, throw open the hand dower and then switch sound and light back to the original machine. It felt like a 30-minute procedure, but it usually took less than a minute.

What did I love about being a projectionist? I loved the smell of the oil and the sound of the machines. I loved knowing when the popcorn downstairs was freshly popped and going down to snag one of the first bags. I loved looking at the people's heads watching the screen. And I loved my fellow projectionists—they were all a bit weird from so many solitary hours in the booth, but they were always open to attempting a bit of human interaction.

I guess that most of all I loved sitting back while the audience below me went through a journey. I felt like the Great Oz, flipping switches and playing with curtains, while the trusting souls below me were transported to magical places. I'd bring down the house lights, fade out the intermission music, and set the stage for an inner journey. Then, when it was over, I'd raise the house lights again and watch the couples and groups and singles walk slowly up the aisles, resuming their outer journey with a fresh and relaxed heart.

Babies are Base 10

B*abies are about as analog* as you can get. As such, they represent a strange new world for those of us used to interfacing with more electronic reality. Having been through the complex transition myself, here are some of my insights, designed to help those of you contemplating the integration of a completely new operating system into your household network.

After living a comfortable life, surrounded by the steady hum of electrons and microprocessors, the erratic upheavals of infancy may seem overwhelming and alien. Indeed, they are. They make no sense whatsoever and should never be perceived as having the least connection to reason. Hence, ***Axiom Number 1: There is no corollary between a baby and logic.*** Standard trouble-shoot-ing procedures will prove futile. Documentation will be faulty, at best. Give it up: the algorithm will change more frequently than the diapers. Do not assume you ever have it wired.

Axiom Number 2: The code gets more complex over time. Moore's law applies to babies as well as to RAM: complexity doubles every 18 months (some would argue every 18 minutes). It's possible—with the help of a few stiff shots of scotch some evening, if you can stay awake long enough—to gain an interesting philosophical perspective on this axiom. It's pretty neat how the programming evolves, develops internal inconsistencies, resolves them, and then develops some more. Strive to achieve this zen-master's appreciation for really sophisticated coding. It will help you through the long days when all you're doing is finding bugs and realize they are all "as designed."

These two axioms understood, here are some tips and terminology that may help you in making the transition to this illogical, unpredictable, and altogether captivating new operating system.

System requirements

Storage space

Storage is going to be an issue from the moment you bring your new system home. Storage needs will be high for the first several years—with an emphasis on portability and rapid access. Storage for the next ten years or so will need to be more robust; you may consider adding on some peripherals, such as bike racks or even a storage shed.

Power

Babies are not terribly efficient processors. The amount of energy these analog systems consume is vastly disproportionate to their size. They seem to tie in to their primary users' energy source and convert it into a seemingly inefficient assemblage of crying, wiggling, excreting and eating. Over time, however, growth patterns do emerge and the energy consumption algorithms become a little more apparent to the naked eye.

Memory

Memory issues with babies are not client-side but more for the server. Unfortunately, they have not yet developed good SIM chips for sleep-deprived parents. Memory (especially short-term) tends to decrease as time goes on, at least until the operating system gets somewhat stable. The key here is to maintain as consistent a buffer as possible. If that is impossible, you may take some comfort in knowing that the problem is usually not terminal; it will resolve itself as soon as more scheduled downtime is available.

Processing speed

Processing speed for babies is not necessarily a benefit. Be aware that, in the beginning, processing speed will be very high for your new system. Nothing you can do will necessarily be able to affect throughput rates, so always be prepared with extra formula or milk and an excess of diapers. You will need both.

Motherboard
A good link with the motherboard is critical to any system's success. Volumes have been written about how best to achieve the maximum in security and reliability. For the novice user, however, just making sure there's a good connection is an excellent start.

Bringing home your new system

Inspecting the hardware
The first thing you'll want to know after your system has been delivered is whether it's functional.

First of all, you'll of course want to make sure it is, indeed, a base 10 system. (Other systems are, of course, adequate, but the base 10 model is by far the industry standard.)

Second, are all fundamental features up to code? You're going to want to make sure the I/O (input/output) systems are in good working order.

Shortly after that, you'll want to plug it into the motherboard. Once that link has been successfully established, you're on your way to developing a long relationship with your new system. (In a few years, you may even want to acquire a new one. See *Timing of Releases*, below.)

Communications protocols

Setting up good communication protocols is essential from the start. Even if the system is operating with a primitive and nearly obsolete language (such as Small-Talk), you need to attempt to interface with it as much as possible. Gradually the system's language will evolve to a point where you will be able to successfully transmit data both ways. Always make sure you interpret the system's messages accurately before responding. This will enable better performance and more accurate troubleshooting.

Monitors

Monitors are useful in the first few months, while you're getting used to how your new system is integrating into your established network. After awhile, however, you may want to operate your system without a monitor, letting independent processing occur without too much direct user intervention.

Operating your new system

Multi-tasking

While your new system will be unable to multitask for quite some time, it is imperative that you, the user, be able to perform several functions at once. This will inevitably include some combination of cooking, holding, feeding and/or changing a diaper. Multitasking generally comes more easily to some users than others, but given enough experience, just about anyone can learn to do it with some degree of grace. Try to avoid over-committing your resources while learning these skills. System overload is a common problem among new users.

Optimizing

To get the best performance out of your system, of course, you will need to balance the I/O (input/output). In the beginning, of course, a solid connection with the motherboard is all your new system is going to need. But over time its needs will become more elaborate. When graduating to more complex input, it is best to add new components gradually, making sure they are compatible with the other elements of the system.

Installing software

Software is vitally important during the first two to three years of your system's life. You can select from two types of software for your new system: cloth (largely obsolete but useful; see *Backing up*, below) or disposable. Be assured, however, that whichever type you select you will be installing and uninstalling software fairly regularly. Unfortunately, experience is the only way to learn successful software techniques; no training manual is ever completely up for the task of demonstrating how to effectively install software.

Backing up

Unlike the binary world, where backing up is a good, preventive maintenance protocol, generally when it comes to babies it's a messy business. Infants back up very often, so it's best to have a good, thick diaper on your shoulder at all times (a good reason to invest in permanent software, even if you don't use it for its intended purpose). Even though the backups are frequent, they are usually benign. The frequency of backups is inversely proportional to their offensive nature; older children, when they do back up, generally do so in a very unpleasant way, and in most inopportune locations. A diaper on your shoulder isn't going to help you one bit after they're about three years old. Sorry.

There are some safety procedures you can initiate to avoid backing up problems. Use common sense when it comes to candy and spinning amusement park rides.

Optimizing your environment

Learning to live with crashes

All systems will crash from time to time. The best thing is to keep a level head when your new system breaks down. Take a moment to assess the severity of the situation. In general, babies are far more robust than computers. Occasionally they will freeze up, but their processors will eventually catch up and you can carry on without any further problem. Be aware that babies VERY seldom "blue screen"—do not attempt to reboot your system on your own! Troubleshoot the situation thoroughly, determine if it's mission critical, and, if it is, take your system into the shop immediately and have a professional technician look at it.

Walking: Is it a bug or a feature?
To the novice, walking appears to be a milestone to be achieved as soon as possible. To the more sophisticated user (usually experienced with one or more releases), walking can easily be perceived as an inherent design flaw.

Unfortunately, the feature is almost always designed into the system, and it's considered a "must have." It's impossible to disable it (without some grievous ethical issues involved) so consider your stance regarding accelerating your implementation of this functionality. It may seem advantageous to hurry the process along, but it contributes exponentially to the instability of the system.

Runtime vs. release version
You can get your system ship-shape, running like a top, perfectly optimized. But bear in mind ***Axiom Number 3: Your system will never perform for outsiders as well as it performs for you***. Just get used to saying things like "Well, it worked at home," and "Funny, I never saw that bug when I was playing with it myself."

Booting up
Booting up—for any kind of extreme weather—has always been an issue in my household. Some systems (usually female ones) actually enjoy booting up, as well as adopting any other kind of adornment. My systems (both male) resent any efforts to change their clothes,

let alone boot up. I find it best to bring an extra set of clothing and shoes and leave rebooting to the demands of discomfort.

Bells and whistles

Bells and whistles (and balls and bats and Hot Wheels tracks) are all very attractive peripherals you will want to invest in. A word to the wise: don't. Try to keep it all to the most minimum. Between grandparents, holidays and birthdays, you will be inundated with all the bells and whistles you can tolerate (see *Storage space,* above).

Scheduling down time

For both you, the user, and your new system, it's imperative that you schedule adequate down time every day. It's not important to do active maintenance during these breaks; internal repairs will be made automatically.

Outsourcing

Everyone needs to outsource from time to time. Some parents will need to give their new system to an outside consultant for much of the workday. Other people will be able to afford part-time contractors. However you work it, relax with the knowledge that your new system will most likely be in fine, competent hands. Remember: most people have been doing this a lot longer than you have. This may not give you a lot of reassurance, but it may help. (Note: try not to dwell on this statement late at night when you are unsure whether your new system has a fever, your spouse is out of town, and the only way to make sure is to take the baby's temperature, the hard way.)

Timing your releases

Multiple versions

Occasionally, you will receive multiple versions of the same system. Twins, triplets and higher multiples can be very rewarding, but often very taxing. Read the sections *Multi-tasking*, *Memory* and *Storage space*, above, carefully.

Early adopters

Early adopters are the venturesome few that will acquire a system type before it's been thoroughly tried out. If you don't have the stomach for such high stakes ventures, watch them carefully, learn from their mistakes, and wait until the mainstream catches up.

The development cycle

Laptop to desktop to tower

Your new analog system is going to scale, whether you like it or not. Be prepared. Your portable little laptop is going to get bulky and unwieldy in short order. You may eventually have a tower on your hands and wonder where the hell it came from. When purchasing clothing, think big. The system will grow. And when giving suggestions for holiday and birthday gifts, always specify a size or two larger than what you're currently using.

Finally, get used to the fact that some of the cutest little duds you've ever seen will only get used once or twice. It's Moore's Law again: system requirements are going to double more rapidly than your ability to keep up with them.

Going public

Eventually, you will want to take your new system out into the world. Good luck. Going public is a risky business and not for the faint-hearted (see *Runtime vs. release version*, above). You will soon learn the best restaurants to take your new system, and you will learn the art of cycling through restaurants so you won't inflict yourselves on the same place too often. It may take years to acquire the art of going public, but when you do, your efforts will be well-rewarded.

Jesus at Two

Every year at advent, there is much talk about the true meaning of Christmas. Symbols abound in the blazing stars, quiet villages, quests for truth. The infant, soft and mild, is tranquility itself. But no one really talks about the years between the birth and adolescence of the Christ child. This year in particular, with my own toddler running around, I've become curious: What was Jesus like in 2 A.D.?

The birth of Jesus has been celebrated for almost two thousand years. Scholars spend lifetimes explaining minute facets of it. But what about the toddler years? I've never heard about His first stumbling steps, that transition from swaddling clothes to underwear, the first time the Holy Baby screamed "Mine!" and then threw Himself on the floor.

Jesus had an unusual situation. Mary and Joseph were, essentially, his foster parents. His Father was away on an extended business trip, and although there was probably some communication, it's a safe bet that physical visitation was limited.

One assumes they got out of that barn situation. And I've never been clear about whether there were any siblings. Let's leave that for scholarly debate. We'll suppose they lived in the suburbs of Bethlehem—a modest, working-class neighborhood. Joseph built his houses, while Mary stayed at home, setting up play dates with other mothers and their kids. What happened the first time that some little Philistine had a special icon that Jesus particularly liked?

It's a tricky situation. Jesus has several options. He could pull it out of the other kid's hand, cast it down, and tell him it's an evil symbol of a soon-to-be dead religion. He could practice a future sermon about loving your enemies. But, maybe the other kid was bigger. Maybe the 'other cheek' business was a bit too sophisticated. Jesus is in a bind. He has to be good, for the rest of civilization. But this is not a very compelling reason for a Toddler. He should have any toy He wants—He's God, for Christ's sake!— and He should have it *now*!

Then he thinks of something. Dad.

His Dad is kind of the Big Guy on the block. Jesus has a fall-back position that really can't be beat. If He really, really wanted to He could smite that nasty little boy down with one well-aimed lightning bolt, and walk away coolly with that nifty icon. What could anyone do? And besides, in thirty-one years they are going to kill Him anyway. There isn't much point to making long-term plans.

Now Dad has His own problems here. If Jesus really gets Himself in trouble, Dad has to come to his rescue. And Jesus knows it. God has to watch His step—or else His only begotten Son is going to end up being a holy terror.

What do you do with a two-year-old deity? Poor Mary. She's the foster mother, given this Child for a few short years, with hardships to endure in the birth department and only vague promises of idolization later. Joseph is probably not much help; not only does he have to work a full time job, he has to watch over some other Guy's kid, and then gets forgotten by almost all the religions ever afterwards. Joseph has always suspected the Immaculate Conception thing anyway.

So Mary's in this situation all alone. What is she supposed to do when the Kid starts wailing? If she smacks Him one, you never know what the real Father is going to do. He sees all, after all. She can try reasoning, but sometimes the little Squirt doesn't want to listen. She cries a cry that has echoed down the centuries: "God is ignoring me! God won't listen to my entreaties!" But in her case, she's just trying to get Him to eat something besides stale Chanukah candy. Prayer and supplication are about all she can resort to. If He listens, she is happy. If not, she wonders what she got herself into. Just like every mother ever in the history of the world.

So Mary copes. Maybe she figures out some games. ("Let's see you walk on some water.") Or maybe she threatens the longest time-out ever—forty days in the wilderness. (He's not up for that yet, but the time will come.) She figures out how to handle this Kid who has been entrusted to her for a few short years. He ruins His appetite. He refuses to brush His teeth. He screams when you mention going to bed. But, eventually, He sleeps.

Mary must look at him then, and sigh with soft relief. The struggles of growing up are temporarily put aside. His ultimate power has been traded in for a few hours of quiet slumber. Mary smiles, wiping the crumbs off His face, and marvels as she does every night ... how her little devil can so immediately turn into a perfect angel.

About the Author

The passion to write has been at the core of Katherine Shirek Doughtie's life since childhood. She grew up in Southern California and left Pasadena immediately after high school.

Katherine worked her way through college, at various times employed as a busboy, waitress, projectionist, legal secretary, stagehand, pizza deliverer and cook. She attended UC Berkeley and Bennington College before receiving a BA in Literature/Creative Writing from UC Santa Cruz. She went on to earn a Masters degree in Screenwriting at UCLA.

After graduate school, Katherine wrote audio adaptations of short stories by Louis L'Amour, produced by Bantam Audio as dramatized books-on-tape. These productions are currently syndicated and being aired on over 100 radio stations nationwide. She wrote several film scripts based on the most successful adaptations.

After starting her family, Katherine began writing essays reflecting her life as a mother of young children and daughter of an aging parent. After her divorce she explored life as a single mother. She has written numerous articles about technical theatre.

Katherine traveled around the world in her early 20s, and has been the technical director for a nationally touring Gilbert & Sullivan opera company since the early 1980's.

Katherine trains in martial arts, practices yoga, and studies a Filipino percussion style called Kulintang. She helps nurture as many passions as possible in her children's lives. She is a seeker of truth, an adventurer of the spirit, and considers that living life mindfully is one of our few true imperatives as human beings.

Discover
Haven Books

www.havenbooks.net

Fiction with vision.
Non-fiction with purpose.

Make Your Reading a Haven!

Audio Books
Audio Dramas

Make Your Listening a Haven!

Haven Books
10153 ½ Riverside Drive, North Hollywood, CA 91602
818/ 503-2518 phone 818/ 508-0299 FAX
info@havenbooks.net